Mark

Be Bamboo AND

be Giraffe!

Chris Juin

6 SECRETS

TO LEVERAGING SUCCESS

A Guide for Entrepreneurs, Family Offices, and Their Trusted Advisors

CHRIS JARVIS, MBA, CFP®

Bestselling Co-Author of *Mastering the Art of Success*

FOREWORD BY **JACK CANFIELD**

A POST HILL PRESS BOOK

6 Secrets to Leveraging Success
A Guide for Entrepreneurs, Family Offices, and Their Trusted Advisors
© 2018 by Chris Jarvis, MBA, CFP
All Rights Reserved

ISBN: 978-1-68261-452-5
ISBN (eBook): 978-1-68261-453-2

Cover design by Ramón E. Peralta, Jr., Peralta Design
Interior design and composition by Greg Johnson, Textbook Perfect

Post Hill Press
New York • Nashville
posthillpress.com

Published in the United States of America

For my late sister Deidre:

*Your challenges inspired me to help those
who struggle to help themselves.*

Contents

Acknowledgments vii

Foreword by Jack Canfield ix

Introduction xii

Chapter 1 **What Kind of Success Are We Trying to Leverage?** 1

Chapter 2 **The Chicken, the Egg, and Your Future** 8

Chapter 3 **The First Secret: Stop Being Beige** 24

Chapter 4 **The Second Secret: *More* Is More—**
Maximize Your Leverage 39

Chapter 5 **The Third Secret: Expect, Prepare for,**
Then Welcome Failure 64

Chapter 6 **The Fourth Secret: Insure Success** 88

Chapter 7 **The Fifth Secret: Leveraging People—**
the Advanced Course 108

Chapter 8 **The Sixth Secret: Be a Legend—Leave a Legacy** 137

Chapter 9 **Follow the Better Path—Now** 158

Additional Resources 160

Acknowledgments

Thank you, Debby Englander. You are a rock star of an editor—offering me guidance, support, and motivation when I need them most. I want to thank Billie Brownell, Devon Brown, and the rest of the team at Post Hill Press, Sarah Heneghan and Alana Mills. You were excited about transforming my idea into reality—and were very patient and understanding when it took me longer than I had hoped.

I want to thank my parents, Dot Fogarty and Ray Jarvis: Thank you for giving me your greatest gifts and your endless love and support. I am lucky to be your child. To my sister, Jennifer Hill, your resilience and creativity are an inspiration. For my wife, Heather, thank you for helping me find a better path to success and happiness. You listen painstakingly to all of my ideas and help me figure out what I need to say, and not say, to connect with the readers I want to reach. For Chloe, Kierstin, and Tyler, thank you for inspiring me to be the best possible father and role model. You make me want to help as many people as I can.

Jason Plummer and Julia Stuart are the backbone of JarvisTower. They take care of the clients and do all of the important work that is discussed in the book. Dan Stanley and Dan Aceti help me better serve my clients. Rod Sager taught me how to work with family offices. Doug Hostetler taught me that the emotional challenges of wealth far outweigh the financial ones. Arlen Brammer is a true friend and valuable legal resource. Mehran Assadi of National Life Group taught me that financial success and social purpose can go hand in hand.

Professors Art Markman and Axel Anderson helped me better understand the scientific and economic elements of the book. Chris Stout-Hazard always gives me excellent advice and helps me stay colorful. Greg Rollett taught me the power of telling my story. Ramón Peralta and the super-fast team at Peralta Design gave me an awesome book cover, website, and social media presence.

Gordon Logan, Rebecca Finell, and Bill Imhoff are true entrepreneurs, mentors, and friends.

Ana Rubio of Streamline Miami, Clayton Frech of Angel City Sports, and Chris Tuffli of Rock and Rock Forever Foundation inspire me with their tireless work to give our children greater opportunities for success.

Jessica Byrne of ODEA Consulting and Jack Canfield coached me through my darkest hours so I could change my mindset, redefine success, and ultimately achieve my highest level of success. Jay Abraham challenged me intellectually and inspired me professionally.

Foreword

by Jack Canfield

When I was searching for industry leaders to contribute their secrets for my new book, *Mastering the Art of Success*, one of my Canfield coaches recommended Chris Jarvis.

Chris submitted a brilliant chapter, titled "Increasing Sales Without Ever Selling." It was not only excellent information for everyone who needs to connect with clients, but it was also very well written. Unsurprisingly, Chris received the Editor's Choice Award from Celebrity Press for his outstanding contribution to the bestselling book.

Later in the year I interviewed Chris for *Hollywood Live*. While in the studio and on air, I was impressed with his ability to simplify and effectively communicate very complicated ideas. During a much longer conversation at dinner that night, we got to know each other better and a genuine connection developed. While we talked, I developed an even deeper respect for his brilliant intellect, his wonderful sense of humor, his no-BS approach to business and life, and his strong commitment to make a difference in the lives of others.

As the co-author of the bestselling *Chicken Soup for the Soul*® series, I have had the opportunity to author or co-author more than 170 books (62 of which are *New York Times* bestsellers). That success has afforded me the opportunity to work with hundreds of thousands of people all over the world, and among all those people, Chris stands out. Unlike many of the people in the financial world, he does not measure his success just by dollars earned. Chris is first and foremost a teacher who wants to help people enjoy their success by eliminating the unnecessary stress and aggravation that often accompany financial success. His motives are pure, and his advice is unbiased.

Chris is an applied mathematician with more than 25 years in financial services. He has worked as an actuary, created over 40 insurance companies, written 15 books, received numerous sales awards, and taught hundreds of seminars to professionals and entrepreneurs. Chris helps entrepreneurs, family offices, law firms, and nonprofit organizations solve their most complicated financial problems.

He is a true industry insider who can teach you the tricks of his most successful clients and can show you how to beat the system by getting firms to work for you, instead of against you.

In this remarkable book, Chris shares the economic data nobody wants you to see. You'll be shocked at how much more money you can make when you figure out how to make your money work better for you. He'll help you see that there is a "crystal ceiling" that keeps those in the top 1% from seeing, let alone experiencing, the higher levels of success that are possible.

Chris shares the two key philosophies that the most successful people in this country always adopt. He'll show you that as soon as you stop trying to fit in, you will have a much better chance of breaking through that crystal ceiling. And once you fully realize that "what got you here won't get you there," you will accept the fact that leverage is the only way to achieve great success. And he offers many practical applications for your consideration.

Chris will show you how his most successful clients set up safety nets so they cannot fail. And with the safety nets, those clients can make riskier bets and enjoy greater rewards. And he'll show you how you too can protect your current success and aim even higher!

As an industry insider, Chris explains how you can transform the costs of insurance and banking into revenue for you, your business, and your family.

Lastly, Chris explains why traditional retirement plans and compensation structures are inadequate for your most valuable people, unappreciated by the rank and file, and detrimental to most companies' balance sheets. He offers valuable insights into the retirement plan of the future. He offers structures that maximize incentives for employees, executives, and advisors while significantly improving the equity of the firm or the long-term endowments of the nonprofit organization or university.

Chris also points out that there are too many people who are rich in spirit but poor in resources, who could help so many more people if they were more financially successful.

Chris also offers a unique perspective on the demographics of the United States, on the financial services industry, and on the biggest influencers of enterprise value. If you know who you are and what you want to do, *6 Secrets to Leveraging Success* will definitely help you elevate your perspective and see a better path to your financial success. And with that financial success, you can choose to become a positive influence in the lives of even more people.

I wish you well on your path to continued and expanded success.

Jack Canfield

Bestselling author of the *Chicken Soup for the Soul*® series and *The Success Principles*™

Introduction

The secret was right under my nose, but I was too busy to notice.

For more than 20 years, I have helped thousands of successful Americans resolve their complicated financial concerns. Making money was not their problem. These were physicians earning millions of dollars, business owners worth tens of millions of dollars, and family offices managing hundreds of millions of dollars.

My challenge was to help them solve the other problems that were keeping them up at night. What kinds of other problems did I unravel? The subjects included lawsuit protection, tax management, retirement, investing, risk management, business succession, and estate planning. I used to say, "You did the hard part. You figured out how to make a lot of money. My job is to help you restructure it so that you get the most enjoyment, and the least aggravation, out of having it." Over time, I saw a pattern of concerns forming. It was my job to find successful people a better path.

Helping successful people mitigate their risks while eliminating unnecessary costs turned out to be a great business model. People are more than willing to spend money to worry less, save money, and enjoy their lives. More valuable than the money is the "shiny new toy" effect. Happy clients really like showing off their creative advisors to their most successful friends. As a result, I got to work with hundreds of businesses *and* their trusted advisors.

While working alongside some of the best attorneys and accountants, I made two very important discoveries. First, I was exposed to strategies and structures that are usually reserved for the largest companies and wealthiest families. These are the tools that help super-charge wealth accumulation and fortify its preservation. Interestingly, the vast majority of financial services professionals are either unaware or choose not to use these amazing strategies. With this set of super tools in my bag, I have been able to build more effective solutions.

Second, and more important, I learned that most work for the wealthiest families is done in silos. The professional firms are so focused on their own expertise, and possibly fearful of the malpractice risk, that they ignore the value of financial or insurance products and strategies in their planning. As a result, the financial plans created solely by tax and legal professionals are also limited. These plans for the very wealthy are typically very costly and unnecessarily less effective than they could be with a minor tweak or two.

Of course, not every advisor is myopic in his or her approach. I am thankful to a number of creative and open-minded professionals who were willing to collaborate with me on some strategies. We created new programs for businesses to create their own insurance companies, for accounting and law firms to eliminate unfunded defined benefit plan liabilities, for nonprofits to eliminate unreasonable compensation, for universities to build their endowments, for private equity firms to boost earnings of portfolio companies, and for family offices to reduce insurance costs for all of their businesses. Though I had found clear paths to success for these clients, something even grander was still eluding me.

Then things started to change. In 2015, my business partner asked me to buy him out of his share of our captive management company, Jade Risk. I was prepared to take on minority partners to help fund this buyout, but things did not go according to plan. The potential acquirers not only asked for controlling interest, but also offered to buy me out completely. I agreed to sell so that I could pay off my investor and put away a sizeable amount of money for myself.

One of the first things I did after the sale was contribute an award-winning segment to Jack Canfield's bestselling book, *Mastering the Art of Success*. Jack, as mentioned in the foreword, is the creator of the

Chicken Soup for the Soul series. It was in my preliminary research for my contribution to that book that I started looking at my own success. As I looked back on my journey and found myself embarking on a new path, I found what had been eluding me.

Like most entrepreneurs, I had worked very hard to get to that moment. During tough times, I put my head down and pushed through the difficulties. I met deadlines, put out fires, and managed very demanding clients and employees. I was so busy doing what needed to be done that I didn't have time to consider why I was doing it in the first place. For the first time in years, I had a chance to reflect on my work, my colleagues, and what I hoped to accomplish with the second half of my life.

As I took a deeper look at the role I had played with my clients, I started to categorize them by size, type of business, and the length of our working relationship. I dug a little deeper and started looking at how much their personal wealth, or the size of their companies, had grown in the years that I had known them. I even took note of their personal philosophies, their views on wealth, and how they structured their advisory teams.

There it was—the unbelievable pattern with my clients that had completely escaped me—until that moment. As an applied mathematician, I couldn't just accept qualitative evidence. I needed to know if the national data were consistent with that of my smaller sample size. I researched and dissected economic reports. I reviewed income tax reports from the Treasury Department. I reviewed the slew of data on income inequality that was released leading up to the presidential election. I looked at the differences among average Americans (the 50th percentile, or 50%), the top 5%, top 1%, top 0.1%, and even the top 0.01%. I learned:

> *What people did to become successful was not as important as what they did after they became successful.*

As with any complex mathematical equation, there are numerous variables that contribute to the outcome. These variables explain why so many people don't reach their desired levels of success and so few do. In *6 Secrets to Leveraging Success*, you will find answers to the following questions:

1. What is the "crystal ceiling" and why is it so important?
2. What institutional, economic, and psychological factors are hindering your success?
3. What "valuable lesson" must you unlearn to be more successful?
4. What are the two most important philosophies of the most successful Americans?
5. How can you eliminate your reliance on the two biggest industries in the world?
6. How do you get employees to act like owners without giving them equity?
7. How do make advisors work for you instead of against you?
8. How do you ensure that your success will help, and not hurt, your family after you are gone?

If you are already successful but just can't seem to get to the next level, *6 Secrets* is for you. If you have followed the advice of your friends and advisors and still haven't reached your goals, *6 Secrets* is for you. If you believe the most successful people in this country are playing by different rules and have an unfair advantage over you, you're right! And *6 Secrets* is going to be both interesting and useful for you.

Please take your time in the early lessons. They will help you understand the competitive landscape. Only one in 500 people earns over $1 million in any given year. Don't think that the other 499 aren't trying! If you don't know what obstacles you are going to face, you are unlikely to be adequately prepared to face them.

After you understand the external challenges you're facing in this economic environment, you will learn what internal challenges successful people face. You will learn how popular philosophies in sociology and psychology explain why it is so difficult to achieve and sustain success. When you can see the external threats all around you and you understand the ones brewing inside of you, you will be better prepared to weather the approaching storm as you set out to take the next steps to reaching higher levels of success.

Once you understand the difficulties of the challenge ahead *and* you prepare yourself to deal with them by eliminating all those false beliefs and detrimental habits, you will be given the practical tools you need to be successful. I will share both philosophical and practical secrets to building wealth, mitigating risk, eliminating unnecessary costs, and turning enemies into allies. With this elevated perspective, you will see a better path to success—and you won't get in your own way any longer.

In the JarvisTower offices, you will see subtle giraffe prints in the upholstery and not-so-subtle giraffe sculptures. The giraffe's elevated perspective and long neck allow it to see and reach things others cannot. This is the same perspective you will have when you finish this book. Please enjoy *6 Secrets to Leveraging Success*, and always remember to elevate your perspective, see a better path, and most important…

Be the giraffe!

Chris Jarvis

P.S. Don't hesitate to reach out to me. I appreciate hearing from readers. I look forward to helping those who want to help themselves. You may email me at chris@jarvistower.com or follow me on Twitter @jarvischris.

CHAPTER 1

What Kind of Success Are We Trying to Leverage?

Given the title of this book, *6 Secrets to Leveraging Success*, it makes sense that we answer the obvious question: what is success? For the purposes of this book, I will do nothing to dispel the myth that every MBA must categorize everything into a 2×2 matrix. There will be two levels of success and two measures of financial success. The levels are very easy to explain—size matters. The categories help us determine what we are measuring. In one category, we measure income or profitability. In the other category, we measure net worth or enterprise value.

	Successful	Most Successful
Income/Profitability (Earners)	$	$$$
Net Worth/Enterprise Value (Accumulators)	$	$$$

Let's consider the four boxes and what their differences are.

Successful Earners—the 1%

Let's define the *successful earners* as individuals who earn more than $400,000 per year. According to Internal Revenue Service reports, earning $400,000 per year represents an income level that fewer than

1% of Americans achieved in 2015. The strategies and philosophies offered in this book have come from people who make much more, often $2 million to $20 million per year. I refer to those with this higher level of income as the *most successful*. *Most* is not the ultimate superlative for our purposes, because there are obviously Americans earning in excess of $20 million per year. I want to make the point that there is a group of people who have achieved an even higher level of success than those in the successful category, so we can look at their qualities as we all try to reach greater levels ourselves.

When I looked at the ideals, characteristics, and strategies of my most successful clients, I found that many of their secrets could be adopted or adapted to fit the needs of entrepreneurs and professionals who earn much less. Looking up to people who have already done what you hope to do is a great strategy in any area of life. In financial planning, it is paramount. If you aren't yet convinced, consider your own life for a moment.

As you reached new levels of income or accumulated greater wealth, did your life become more or less complicated? Greater success brings about financial challenges that require more specialized attention. Your business may take on investors. You may pay more in estimated quarterly tax payments than you earned in your first three years of working—combined! You will have a detailed chart that accompanies your personal financial statement. Somehow, this combination of boxes, arrows, and tiny footnotes is supposed to save you time—and it doesn't. Your children's marriages will cause you to question, if not obsess over, how you can protect any inheritance you may leave.

The most successful regularly face these problems. In some cases, families have had multiple generations to sort out the best ways to manage them. The important lesson is that you must accept the fact that you will have problems, challenges, and setbacks (see the third secret for powerful philosophies and practical strategies). The secret to long-term and sustained success is to implement strategies before the problems arise. Before we move on to those valuable ideas, let's consider the other category of success.

Successful Accumulators—Millionaires

For this book, a *successful accumulator* is a person or family with a current or projected net worth in excess of $1 million. This is a simple calculation of net worth as the sum of total assets less the total of liabilities and debts. Even in 2017, if you are a millionaire, we can safely call you successful. Because of the unique family dynamic and the challenges it may cause to successful accumulators, I use the term *successful families* interchangeably with *successful accumulators* throughout the book.

Though you would be impressed by the average net worth of my current clientele, it would be highly misleading (when you read chapter 2, you will learn why). Most of my experiences in the past ten years have been with families that have a net worth between $10 million to $100 million. This has taught me a great deal about the mental, financial, and emotional challenges of successful accumulators. This book is the product of my eye-opening client experiences. I have had the pleasure of working with multiple families worth hundreds of millions of dollars, and with two billionaires and their dedicated family offices. I have seen a significant difference in how the wealthier families manage wealth. For that reason, we will define the *most successful* among the accumulators as families that have a net worth in excess of $50 million.

Successful accumulators have many of the same challenges that successful earners have. The big difference is that successful families are most concerned with transferring wealth to future generations, making tax-efficient charitable contributions, and building an organizational legacy. The most successful of these families have these same concerns, but the amounts are obviously much more significant. As a result, they generally make a much more concerted effort to address legacy building in their planning. Many of the most powerful strategies are covered in the sixth secret. Before you learn the best ways to leave your mark on the planet after you are gone, you may want to work through the first five secrets to see how you can get the most out of your success during your lifetime.

You Can Be Both

Many people obviously fall into both categories. If you are a successful earner and you don't spend all your money on bad investments, overpriced entertainment, or your children, you will become a successful accumulator just by grinding it out long enough. Conversely, even if you became a successful accumulator the old-fashioned way—you inherited it—you have to do something with your money. If you were not the unmotivated child and you learned something about leverage from someone along the way, you likely are a successful earner as well.

Keep in mind that being both a successful earner and a successful accumulator is not a given. Let's take my friend Bret Williams as an example.

■ **CASE STUDY**

Be Neither. Be One. Be Both. Be One Again

Bret Williams was the CEO of The Vermont Hard Cider Company. He helped build the Woodchuck Cider brand into a market leader. While building the company, he put much of his income back into the company to build the brand. For years, he worked hard but was not highly successful based on the definitions in this chapter. When the company became profitable, Bret started to make some money. He didn't have a lot of cash, but his wealth was tied up in a company that might have been worth $25 million. He had investors and other executives who owned the company with him, but there was no real opportunity to sell the company.

As gluten-free products started to become popular in America, the Woodchuck brand exploded. (Unlike beer, cider is naturally gluten-free.) In 2012, the C&C Group of Ireland purchased the company for $305 million. Instantly, Bret was in the category of most successful accumulators mentioned earlier. He stayed on with C&C after the merger to help with the integration—making him a successful earner, too. After 18 months of working with the new company, Bret did what many executives do: he stepped down. At that point, he was technically unemployed. He was most successful in terms of his acquisition of wealth, but he had no income. This is just one case of someone who saw his status (based on our simplified metrics) change four times in three years.

For a less extreme and more likely scenario, consider a surgeon or an attorney who has finally become a partner at a medical practice or law firm. The physician might see a significant bump in income, but might defer much of those funds to buy into the very profitable surgery center or hospital. Student loans might still need to be paid too. Though the gross income might be $1 million or more, the physician might have a negative net worth. It would seem inaccurate to categorize him or her as unsuccessful when that hospital or surgery center investment and medical practice income may throw off $25 million in earnings over the next 20 to 30 years.

Similarly, an attorney may be out celebrating the promotion to partner at an Am Law 200 firm, and a salary (plus projected partner bonus) that went from $450,000 to $1 million per year. Though that income is very high, the attorney is now a partner who is on the hook for the firm's unfunded defined-benefit plan for its soon-to-be-retiring Baby Boomer partners. The firm also may owe hundreds of millions of dollars to its senior partners. Is it possible that becoming partner just caused the attorney's net worth to drop? Consider the following data.

According to JarvisTower's contacts at two of the largest banks in America—who work with most of the large law firms—the equity partners of law firms could be considered "liability partners." This is because many firms are sitting on substantial liabilities that will eventually be paid out to the older partners. Using traditional financial valuation models, many of the most prestigious firms may have a negative value on the balance sheet. This is certainly the case if you exclude the value of their intangible goodwill. (These firms are my clients, so you will have to insert your own paradoxical joke about goodwill and lawyers here.) The unique challenges facing physicians, accountants, and attorneys are outside the scope of this book, but they are covered slightly in the fifth secret. For a more detailed explanation of the problems and more creative solutions, readers of 6 Secrets can download a special report, "Partnership Pitfalls: Creative Solutions for Accountants, Attorneys and Physicians," at JarvisTower.com/resources.

Why Big Earners Fail to Accumulate

Though it is true that successful earners often become successful accumulators, this does not apply at higher levels of success. The most successful accumulators did not generally get there by becoming most successful earners. When you fall into the trap of "working harder" to get to the higher level of success, you are severely stunting your financial growth. There are only so many hours in the day. If you did four deals, saw 4,000 patients, or drafted 50 sets of legal documents last year and made $1 million, you had a great year. However, you could fall into the trap of believing that you could kill yourself and do eight deals, see 8,000 patients, or draft 100 sets of documents and double your income. You are half right. You would kill yourself trying, but you just won't get there. Doing it yourself and "working harder" are not smart ways to become one of the most successful. This lesson will be demonstrated throughout the rest of the book.

Review the Matrix

Throughout the book, you will see countless references to the successful and the most successful. The following grid specifies the monetary characteristics of each group.

	Successful	**Most Successful**
Income/Profitability	>$400,000/year	$2 million–$20 million/year
Net Worth/Enterprise Value	>$1 million	>$10 million

In most cases, the successful are the people reading this book who are hoping to achieve a higher level of success. The most successful will often be referred to as the people who have already cleared the path to success. Unlike otherwise noted, the lessons throughout the book came from my most successful clients.

See Your Better Path

You are more than likely successful in your own right. But you just aren't where you want to be. It's easy to comprehend that success can be measured by your W-2 or 1099 or personal financial statement. When you see people sitting courtside at the NBA finals, see someone driving a new $300,000 Bentley SUV, or hear about someone's $100 million charitable gift, you know that these are not average people. These occurrences should make it obvious that there is a much higher level of wealth achieved by some people in our country. Until now, there has not been a book that shares the different philosophies and offers practical strategies to help you, the successful, change your current situation and see what you can do differently to achieve those higher levels of success.

Before I tell you the secrets of the most successful, it is imperative to understand what external challenges exist for you. Once you understand why so few people achieve those levels of success you desire, we can proceed to the single most important concept regarding success: leverage. When you understand why it is hard to succeed, and you decide to set big goals anyway, you have taken the first step. When you understand and embrace the fundamental concept of leverage, you then have the right mindset to reach your goals. Then, you will be ready to review the practical strategies that will help you get there.

CHAPTER 2

The Chicken, the Egg, and Your Future

Which came first, the chicken or the egg? This is the classic causality dilemma: either answer could be correct. Did something other than a chicken lay an egg that developed into a chicken? Did a chicken lay the first egg as a different form of reproduction? Questions like this one take researchers, the curious, and the argumentative down a path of causality. Did the chicken cause the creation of eggs or did an egg cause the creation of chickens?

You don't have to be a Beatle to be an egg man (or to be a walrus). Some scientists contend that the egg must have come first. There were apparently direct ancestors of the modern chicken that did indeed produce eggs. Perhaps enough genetic mutations created the first modern chicken from two non-chicken parents.

On the other hand, the sky won't necessarily fall if you have a different opinion. My little chicken is my nine-year-old daughter, Chloe. She overheard me discussing the idea for this chapter. She quickly jumped in and said, "There's no dilemma. God created all the animals, including the chickens. The chicken came first." Apparently, there are adults who also believe in the concept of creationism.

In the third camp, there are the pain-in-the-ass folks who think that this is merely a question of semantics. They say that since the chicken is mentioned before the egg, the answer is simply that the chicken came before the egg.

You may be wondering what *caused* me to include a chicken-and-egg piece in a book about the secrets to success. You might be asking yourself if this chapter is the *effect* of an exhausted or hallucinating author's attempt to get the book to his publisher on time. Rest assured, those concerns need not be mutually exclusive. If you indulge me, I will make a connection between the chicken-and-egg question and a very popular theory about money. Since money is the unit of measurement for income and wealth, it is often a proxy for success.

What Comes First, Having Money or Making Money?

As with the chicken and the egg, the "having" versus "making" money question is another causality dilemma. Most people can appreciate that either could come first. Let's look at some direct and indirect ways that each of these two paths can be correct before I offer suggestions for leveraging your own situation.

Let's start with the oldest recorded way to "have" money—through an inheritance. Monarchies would hand down wealth and power to the next generation. Having a crown, a treasure chest, and an army seems like one hell of a head start. Contrast a royal upbringing to that of a peasant. Royals contemplate how to take over new lands or how to open valuable trade routes. Members of the working class must get up early and work their farms from dawn to dusk just to be able to feed the family and pay the tariffs. They are so busy that they have precious little time for planning. The only opportunity for leverage is perhaps having oxen to help with the heavy workload.

Though the challenges of the poor haven't changed much, the opportunities for leveraging money certainly have. You don't need to be given a kingdom to get a head start. There are many ways that successful families can, and do, help their children. The good old-fashioned inheritance is an obvious one. According to research by the Spectrum Group, as cited by Bloomberg, over 73% of surveyed investors under age 50 with assets above $25 million said an inheritance factored into their success. Long before the inheritance, families who "have money" generally give their children a superior education. This can lead to higher-paying jobs and increased opportunities for professional advancement. With greater income, the children will *make* more money. All things being equal, earning more will cause them to eventually *have* even more.

You have undoubtedly heard the phrase "It takes money to make money." This adage appears to be universally accepted. The phrase supports the idea that you must have money to be able to make money. The questions that anyone seeking to earn more money should be asking are:

1. How important is it to save and reinvest my earnings?

2. What can I do if I am not making much money now?

In this chapter, I will prove (mathematically) that having money does in fact allow you to make more money. More important, you will learn how much more money your money will make for you as you climb each rung of the socio-economic ladder.

While everyone with a Twitter handle or YouTube channel hopes to break the internet, mathematicians dream of gaining notoriety from breaking (disproving) a universally accepted theorem or law. Those exceptions to the rule (that you must first have money to make money) could be the keys to unlocking the wealthiest Americans' secrets to success.

TABLE 1: How to Interpret Income Percentile Charts

Category	How many Americans reach this level?
Bottom 90%	This group represents the 9 out of 10 people who didn't reach the next level (the top 10% of earners).
Top 10%	1 out of every 10 people reaches this level.
Top 1%	1 out of every 100 people reaches this level.
Top 0.1%	1 out of every 1,000 people reaches this level.
Top 0.01%	1 out of every 10,000 people reaches this level.

Spoiler alert: if there weren't ways to make money without first having money, there wouldn't be many pages in this book!

How Much Money Do Americans Make?

As a mathematician, I pride myself on making sure that the numbers I share are accurate. Can you imagine any scenario in which a news or reporting organization would alter, massage, or misrepresent data to further a particular agenda? Imagine my surprise when I started doing research for this book and the income and wealth data I found were inconsistent, inaccurate, or inexplicable. None of the numbers matched across multiple sources.

Luckily, I was able to turn to a longtime friend of mine, Axel Anderson, PhD, a professor of economics at Georgetown University. He and I went to Classical High School (in Providence, Rhode Island) together. Axel pointed me to the award-winning research of Emmanuel Saez, professor of economics at University of California, Berkeley. What I found was very helpful. Consider Table 2:

TABLE 2: Income Distribution (Including Realized Capital Gains)

Percentile threshold (1)	Income threshold (2)	Income groups (3)	Number of families (4)	Average income in each group (5)
Bottom 90%	$0	Bottom 90%	150,582,600	$34,074
Top 10%	$124,810	Top 10%–1%	15,058,260	$195,709
Top 1%	$442,900	Top 1%–0.1%	1,505,826	$765,815
Top 0.1%	$2,045,000	Top 0.1%–0.01%	150,583	$3,984,218
Top 0.01%	$11,267,000	Top 0.01%	16,731	$31,616,431
		Total	167,314,000	$61,920

Let's start by explaining this chart's information. Columns 1 and 2 go together. As an example, only 10% of American families earn more than $124,810. Only 1% of American families (one out of every 100) earn more than $442,900 per year. Only 0.01% (one in 10,000 families) earn more than $11,267,000 per year. As you can see, the income numbers increase substantially with each jump.

Columns 3, 4, and 5 should be looked at together. This is an ingenious dissection of data by Dr. Saez. He is considering the bottom 90% of each grouping, to eliminate any distortion in the data that might have resulted from the inclusion of the very high earners in the group. Consider the following: Bill Gates and nine schoolteachers are standing together onstage. I could say that the average net worth of the group members was approximately $9 billion. That would be accurate but very misleading. You might think that all ten are billionaires, but the reality is that Bill Gates is worth $87 billion.

Let's look at the Top 10% row in Table 2. Column 3 includes the row Top 10%–1%. Read that as "the top 10% minus the top 1%." This group includes families who earn more than $124,910 per year, but excludes the top 10% of that group, who earn more than $442,900. This is a group of 15 million families with an average income of $195,709. If you look in the next row, you will see the top 1% minus the top 0.1%. There are over 1.5 million families earning more than $442,900 and less than $2,045,000 per year. The average income of this group is $765,815.

Please bear with me. I promise there won't be a test. You don't need to understand how to create the tables. Once we get through two more short tables, you may not even have to understand the tables in their entirety. I will call out all the important observations that are necessary to make my point. That being said, what are the big takeaways from the chart?

First, the average American family earns $61,920 per year. This number is italicized in the last row and last column of the table. Many successful people I know think $62,000 is a modest but livable income. I must confess that even I, a mathematician who should have known better, fell victim to the data-distortion trap. I blindly accepted the average income number to reflect the "average" American family's earnings. I have quoted that average income number to my children on numerous occasions to try to demonstrate that our lives are privileged and something to be appreciated. My kids gave those conversations as much credence as I gave my father's "I walked five miles to school in the snow, uphill both ways" stories.

When I looked at the data from Dr. Saez, I was shocked to see the impact the top 10% of earners had on it. In the top row of data in the table, you can see that the bottom 90% of American families earn an average of $34,074. I found that number to be disturbingly low. I don't know anyone who believes $34,000 is a reasonable income. I am not going to jump into a discussion about income inequality in America. That is not the topic for this book. I merely share this example to show you how "average income" statistics can be very misleading when you include outliers. Removing those outliers will help you gain a better appreciation for what is actually happening behind the data.

Next, you may want to look at the income numbers at the higher end of the table. In the row titled Top 1%, you will see that only one in 100 families (there are over 1.5 million of them) earns more than $442,900 per year. Further, only one in 10 of those who earn more than $442,000 earns over $2 million per year. Those are the 0.1%. The target market for this book is the 1% who earn more than $442,000 who want to become even more successful. Let's learn how to do that.

How Much Money Does It *Really* Take to Make More Money?

Table 2 includes taxable income: earned income, passive investment income, and realized capital gains (assets sold for a profit). Dr. Saez went a step further and removed the investment gains from the table. In Table 3 on the next page, you will see how much income is generated from labor and passive investments in each class.

Unsurprisingly, Table 3 has lower numbers than Table 2, because realized capital gains were removed. I won't waste your time summarizing this table like I did the previous one—partly because I don't want to bore you and partly because I'm running out of space in this chapter. What is more important for all of us to consider is what was removed from the previous table to generate this one. The difference between the numbers in the two tables is the investment gain for each group. This is the value that previously accumulated wealth generated by being reinvested for the families' benefit. See Table 4.

TABLE 3: Income Distribution (Excluding Realized Capital Gains)

Percentile threshold (1)	Income threshold (2)	Income groups (3)	Number of families (4)	Average income in each group (5)
Bottom 90%	$0	Bottom 90%	150,582,600	$33,219
Top 10%	$121,810	Top 10%–1%	15,058,260	$187,226
Top 1%	$407,760	Top 1%–0.1%	1,505,826	$670,188
Top 0.1%	$1,635,100	Top 0.1%–0.01%	150,583	$2,906,694
Top 0.01%	$7,474,600	Top 0.01%	16,731	$18,862,641
		Total	**167,314,000**	**$57,281**

TABLE 4: Realized Capital Gains (aka Investment Income) by Group

Percentile threshold (1)	Average income in each group (2)	Realized capital gains (3)	Capital gains as % of income (4)	Capital gains as multiple of bottom 90% income (5)
Bottom 90%	$33,219	$855	2.6%	0.026
Top 10%	$187,226	$8,463	4.5%	0.26
Top 1%	$670,188	$95,627	14.3%	2.9
Top 0.1%	$2,906,694	$1,077,524	37.1%	32.4
Top 0.01%	$18,862,641	$12,753,790	67.6%	384.9
Total	**$57,281**	**$4,639**	**8.1%**	

So, not only does income grow exponentially as you move into the higher threshold, but the investment income grows too. Look at the top 1% as an example. That group earns $95,627 of realized capital gains. That is 14.3% more income for the people in that group, over their active income, each year. Although 14.3% may not sound like a lot, it equates to almost three years of pre-tax income for the average family in the bottom 90%. *That* is a lot of money. Imagine how much easier your life could be if you had three additional years' worth of income this year!

If you look at the top 0.1%—the level of income that only one in 1,000 people achieve—the numbers are more staggering. That group of people earns nearly $3 million per year. In addition, they earn over $1 million per year in capital gains. The investment amount, which is symbolic of the profit they have earned on their savings, is equivalent to 32.4 years of income for the average family in the bottom 90%.

In Einstein's later years of life, he was asked, "What is the most powerful force on earth?" He responded, "The power of compound interest!" The more you can earn, the more you can save. The more you save, the more you invest. The more you invest, the more it compounds into a legacy. The numbers from Dr. Saez prove this point decades later. How could anyone possibly argue that money doesn't help you earn more money?

Before we get into the exceptions to the rule, let's explore how the "averages" offered above vary in different parts of the country. We'll take a look at some geographic variations for comparison purposes and see what valuable lesson can be learned.

Location, Location, Location— Where You Live Matters

We just looked at the disparities in income nationwide. This tells only part of the story. There are significant disparities in income from state to state. This is an important variable, because it takes surplus income to be able to make money *on* your money. You can create more investment leverage if you can earn more or spend less.

Consider the minimum income threshold to be included in the top 1% of earners in each state. On the left side of Table 5, you will see the ten states with the highest minimum income thresholds to be in the top 1% of all earners in that state. On the right side, you can see the states with the lowest qualifying income thresholds to be in the top 1% of earners in those states.

TABLE 5: What Do the Top 1% Earn in Each State?

State/District	At Least	State	At Least
Connecticut	$678,000	Arkansas	$228,000
District of Columbia	$555,000	New Mexico	$241,000
New Jersey	$539,000	West Virginia	$243,000
Massachusetts	$532,000	Mississippi	$263,000
New York	$506,000	Kentucky	$263,000
North Dakota	$502,000	Alabama	$272,000
California	$438,000	Maine	$274,000
Illinois	$424,000	South Carolina	$275,000
Texas	$423,000	Hawaii	$279,000
Maryland	$419,000	Idaho	$280,000

Source: Adapted from Estelle Sommeiller and Mark Price's "The Increasingly Unequal States of America: Income Inequality by State," 1917 to 2012, an Economic Analysis and Research Network (EARN) report, January 26, 2015; go.epi.org/unequalstates.

To make sure you are reading the table properly, I offer this brief explanation. In Connecticut, one in every 100 residents earns at least $678,000 per year. By sharp contrast, only 1% of Arkansas residents earn more than $228,000.

At first glance, most of the data in Table 5 makes perfect sense. You would expect there to be a lot of people living in and around New York who have very high salaries—making the top 1% threshold quite high. You were probably unsurprised by the low thresholds in many of the Southern states—where the cost of living is much lower.

What is the takeaway? From the previous section, you learned that the higher-income families boost their incomes significantly (37% to 67%) through their investments. Contrast that with the 99% of Americans who earn less than 5% of their income from their investments. Think of earning money as the chicken and investing money as the egg. You can't be 100% sure which one must come first, but you do understand that the more you earn, the more you can invest. You also understand that the more investments you make, the more likely you are to earn more. Don't think of this as a vicious cycle. Think of this as Einstein's beloved power of compounding.

If you truly want your money to make money for you, the first key is to spend less than you earn. In my experience working with clients who have a very high net worth, there are two formulas for sustained success:

1. You can be a big earner in a location with a low cost of living; or
2. You can be a frugal spender in a high-cost-of-living locale.

Dr. John. Dr. John is an orthopedic surgeon in upstate New York. He is worth upwards of $50 million. When I asked him how he is worth so much, he told me that he "lives small." He has earned around $1 million per year for 30 years, but that is a small piece of the equation. Since he is paid by insurance payers, he earns a similar amount per procedure as his colleagues in much more expensive places to live. By living in Buffalo, he was able to buy a nice home worth less than $500,000. He says that it costs him less to take his wife, three children, their spouses, and his half-dozen grandkids to brunch every Sunday than it costs him to take his medical school buddy to lunch in Manhattan. His strategy was to live in a smaller town with less aggravation, lower expenses, and less competition.

Bret the Beverage Guy. Bret built a business in Vermont producing gluten-free alcoholic cider. Though Vermont is not easily accessible from any major city, he was able to leverage a number of things. He had lower labor costs and could buy less expensive real estate. These lower costs allowed him to ramp up his production and take advantage of the growing interest in adult cider. With his savings, he was also able to increase distribution and gain a significant market share. This investment in infrastructure was a gamble, but it paid off significantly. The spike in gluten allergies and celiac disease caused gluten-free cider to take off! After one failed attempt to gain access to the US cider market, an Irish beverage giant chose to buy Bret's company for over $300 million. Bret's leverage of his lower costs allowed him to achieve massive distribution. This made him a very attractive acquisition target. The owners and investors were very well rewarded.

Dr. David. Dr. David is a plastic surgeon in Northern California. He reluctantly left the beautiful Palo Alto area for a much smaller town halfway between the Bay Area and Reno. With much less competition, he was able to increase his income from $450,000 per year to over $1 million by his second year. By reinvesting the surplus into his practice and real estate, he was able to double his income again. How many of his Bay Area friends have a 7,000-square foot, six-bedroom home in a gated community, a ski chateau, millions of dollars' worth of investments, and very little traffic to negotiate?

Stan the Understated. I recall the day I drove up from Austin, Texas, to meet Stan at his home outside Dallas. As I was walking up to his home, I thought to myself, "My house is so much nicer than Stan's." I then stopped dead in my tracks. Stan's house was understated on the outside. There was no big curb appeal, like I had in the hills of Austin. However, inside the home, Stan had artwork that was worth more than my very expensive home. Stan also had two other properties, investment real estate worth millions, a private jet, and over $30 million in net worth. He didn't care what other people thought about his wealth. He was focused on buying things that his family and friends would see and enjoy. By focusing on practical purchases and ignoring the status symbols, he was able to amass a fortune when others in his field were worth 10% what he was.

Basically, if you need to brag about where you live or show off how you live, you will never have any money left to leverage. In the second secret, you will learn just how powerful leverage is, so we won't spend more time on it now. It's important to point out that there is only so much you can sacrifice to get ahead. Buying smaller homes and going on fewer vacations will get you only so far. There is a much bigger philosophy for you to adopt if you are ever going to break through the crystal ceiling (which I will explain shortly).

The Exception: You *Can* Beat the Odds

We have discussed how having money not only helps you make more money, but helps you more and more as you continue to increase your earnings. We know that the exponential power is something we all hope to harness. The first question is, can it be done?

On November 31, 2016, *Fortune* magazine published an article titled "1,700 People in America are Becoming Millionaires Every Day." This information was shared from a Bloomberg report that was based on projections from the Boston Consulting Group. Earlier in the chapter, we mentioned another report from Bloomberg, regarding the Spectrum Group's research on investors under 50 years of age with assets greater than $25 million. It said that 73% of respondents cited inheritance as a factor in their success. Though that is a large percentage, this is very encouraging to those of us who don't believe we have an inheritance coming our way, because it means 27% of investors with more than $25 million in assets didn't see inheritance as a factor! In my head, I am hearing Jim Carrey's character Lloyd Christmas in *Dumb and Dumber* saying, "So you say I have a chance?"

In addition, at the highest end, there are still new entries. *Forbes* reported on March 20, 2017, that there were 195 new billionaires in the world in 2017. In June 2017, lovemoney.com reported a record 233 new entries to the billionaire club.

It's not just a gray-hair club either. You don't have to be old to be rich and successful. Consider Table 6 on the following page, a short list of self-made young billionaires.

This information should be very encouraging. You can become very successful by a very young age. You can even become a billionaire if you don't have a lot of money. If these "youngins" can acquire their wealth with fewer than 15 years of adulthood, you should realize that this journey doesn't have to be an epic one that will take an entire lifetime. Let's look at the statistical and anecdotal evidence that supports the changes needed for you to achieve those higher levels of success, and I'll discuss the important concept of the crystal ceiling.

TABLE 6: Young Self-Made Billionaires

Name	Age	Net Worth	Source
Mark Zuckerberg	33	$56 billion	Facebook
Dustin Moskovitz	33	$10.7 billion	Facebook/Asana
Bobby Murphy	28	$4 billion	Snap Inc.
Evan Spiegel	27	$4 billion	Snap Inc.
Nathan Blecharczyk	34	$3.8 billion	Airbnb
John Collison	26	$1.1 billion	Stripe
Patrick Collison	28	$1.1 billion	Stripe

Source: Created from data in *Celebrity Money*, June 15, 2017, and *MSN Money*, June 6, 2017.

What Is the Crystal Ceiling?

The crystal ceiling is the not-so-imaginary difference between the top 1% of earners and the top 0.1% of earners in the United States. The crystal ceiling is very different from the glass ceiling. With a glass ceiling, you can see the job you want, but there is some invisible barrier stopping you from achieving it. It could be race, gender, creed, or some other element that leads to discrimination. For the crystal ceiling, think about an ornate cut-crystal glass or decanter you may have held in your hand. Yes, it's fancier than glass, but that is not the point. The ornate features allow you to see the color of the beverage inside the glass, but you certainly wouldn't want to try to read something through the crystal. The crystal ceiling is a similar concept, as the average American really can't really see what life looks like on the other side. Even those successful people who earn at least $440,000 per year don't have any idea how to raise their incomes to $2 million, $4 million, or $11 million per year.

There is no clear career path or investment opportunity to break through the crystal ceiling and get to the levels of success that only one in 1,000, or one in 10,000, Americans will achieve. Axel explained it so simply to me: "You can only earn so much with labor. You need some serious luck, or a lucky set of circumstances, to get to the highest levels of income."

Consider this rather unscientific but simple experiment. You don't need to be very wealthy to know who makes $400,000 per year. The named partner at the law firm, the surgeons and other medical specialists in your town, and even the car dealer who has a few dealerships earn at least $400,000. You can see that a successful business owner or someone with a professional degree can get to that 1% threshold.

At the other end of the spectrum, it shouldn't be too hard to fathom how someone who earns $4 million can increase income to $11 million per year. That person has a ton of money and doesn't need most of it to support the cost of living, and is investing all over the place. Everyone seems to accept the fact that it takes money to make money. If you are one of the wealthiest people in your city or town, you will have an unending number of opportunities to invest in things others simply can't afford. If you have favorable results with those investments, your income will continue to grow.

Getting out of the top 1% is really hard to comprehend. There are a lot of people who earn $400,000 per year. According to the Tax Policy Center, there are 1,128,000 taxpayers in this group. If you believe that statistic, then you should accept the center's estimate that there are 115,000 people who earn more than $10 million per year. If you add up all the professional athletes in the United States, you'll find there are fewer than 10,000 of them. I estimate that 10% of the athletes earn more than $10 million per year. Aha! We just found 1,000 of the 115,000 we were hoping to identify. Where are the other 114,000 people who earn $10 million per year? I am in the high-net-worth space as a sought-after advisor. I have probably met 100 to 200 of them. With that unique experience, I still can't tell you where to easily locate any large groups of those big earners in any state, let alone in yours.

Axel's statement is the key to this book. There is no clear, simple path to reaching the highest levels of success. However, there *are* two very important philosophies that are common among the most successful people on this planet. These two concepts are, unsurprisingly, the first and second secrets to leveraging success.

Once you understand, appreciate, and embrace the two most important philosophies to success, you will be ready to move on from intellectual motivation to practical application. There are four innovative financial strategies that can be utilized to increase personal wealth or enhance enterprise value. Family offices, public companies, start-ups, and private investors have successfully utilized these strategies. As you read them, keep an open mind. Most of these strategies can be altered to fit your specific situation—so you can achieve your goals sooner than you may have thought possible.

See a Better Path

This chapter opened by asking which came first, the chicken or the egg? We then migrated to a different dilemma—does it really take money to make money? We not only demonstrated that the existence of surplus income leads to even more surplus, but we also quantified how much more money certain segments of the US population are gaining from their investments. On average, people earn 8% of their income from investments, but the wealthiest one in 1,000 Americans gains 36% to 67% more income from investments. The takeaway is that money *does* make more money.

You saw examples of very successful people who took the lower-profile approach to grow their wealth. By choosing to live in less expensive areas, they saved more money. This allowed them to invest in their businesses and to invest in real estate—both of which helped increase their incomes even further. Texans refer to showy wealth as "big hat, no cattle." If you are spending a lot of time showing off, you probably don't have much left to back it up.

Most important for most of you, you saw examples of self-made billionaires who are under the age of 40. You don't in fact need to have money to make money. You don't even need to have money to make a billion dollars in less than ten years. You can make a lot of money, and you can make it in a relatively short time—with some luck, some dedication, and a whole new mindset about money.

You learned about the crystal ceiling. There is an awareness of families that are worth hundreds of millions of dollars, but there is absolutely no road map for the rest of us to get there. We can't idolize them, because we can't see them clearly. They are on the other side of the crystal ceiling. This is an invisible but very real set of economic, psychological, and social factors that keep all of us from reaching this much desired level of income.

You learned how the low-expense lifestyle is only one way to grow wealth—and a completely unacceptable one to anyone whose company or industry is located on one of the coasts or in a major metropolitan area. Those people have to embrace a new mental approach, and they have to execute new strategies if they are going to reach higher levels of success.

Those who have catapulted their way from the top 1% into the top 0.1% have not done it by following any playbook. If there were a playbook, everyone in the top 1% would be at the 0.1% level—and that is mathematically impossible. The most successful people in our country achieved that level of success because they saw an opportunity that others didn't. Their elevated perspective allowed them to see a better path, by doing something nobody had ever done before or by doing something others do but much better, faster, or more cheaply.

Once you accept and appreciate that there is a crystal ceiling, you'll learn the internal and external factors that contribute to its existence. Most important, this book will share with you six practical steps you can take to break the crystal ceiling and turn *your* champagne wishes and caviar dreams into reality (said in my best Robin Leach accent).

To get to that higher level of success, you will have to do something radically different. If you accept Maslow's hierarchy of needs, you might believe that only crazy people can actually achieve those higher levels of success. Please continue on to the first secret to leveraging success: Stop Being Beige. You will learn why you can't be boring and why you can't second-guess yourself on your way to achieving your desired level of success.

CHAPTER 3

The First Secret:
Stop Being Beige

You are undoubtedly reading this book because you want to achieve a greater level of success. If your goal is to earn over $1 million per year, you have set your sights on reaching an income level that only one in every 1,000 people achieves. More ambitious goals may be associated with success that only one in 10,000 people reaches. Obviously, what you are hoping to accomplish is something that a precious few ever do.

After seeing the demographic and economic statistics in the previous chapters, you have to appreciate that the numbers are not in your favor. Henry Ford once said, "Whether you think you can or you think you can't, you're right!" If you remain committed to your goals and you continue to seek contrarian advice (from this book or other sources), you will learn what you have to do to beat the odds and reach those higher levels of success.

Throughout this book I will offer practical lessons, each of which has multiple ideas that you may integrate. But before you can move on to those, you have to learn the first secret to achieving the highest levels of success. This lesson is fundamental to everything else in this book. I have learned this important lesson from decades of working with some of the most successful families and entrepreneurs in this country.

A truly entrepreneurial furniture designer in Omaha, Nebraska, best summarized this lesson for me. Chris Stout-Hazard is a longtime friend of mine who has helped me in many of my endeavors. Before starting his company, which focuses on custom American-made furniture, with his husband, Roger Hazard (a designer and a television presenter on A&E's *Sell This House*), Chris helped me build an investment firm, a publishing company, an insurance agency, a financial fellowship for physicians, and an insurance management and consulting shop. He and Roger are currently helping us with interior and exterior designs for a home-building project in Southlake, Texas. Their company is called Roger + Chris (www.rogerandchris.com).

Chris has a wide range of skills, and he definitely understands my eccentricities. This is why I run all of my crazy ideas by him before jumping in with two feet. During a recent conversation, Chris told me something about decorating that turned out to be much more profound than I realized at the time. When discussing color schemes, he said:

> *"The more people you ask for a color suggestion, the more likely you are to end up with beige."*

He went on to say, "When you ask a group of people to make a decision, you inevitably end up with each person agreeing to something he doesn't hate. Nobody gets to choose anything that he loves. We all just agree on something that nobody hates. It's beige. It's boring. It's safe. It sucks."

Chris continued with the analogy. "Consider what every real estate agent recommends to a home seller: 'You should paint the entire house a neutral color.' Wait for it…maybe beige? The idea is to make sure the color does not influence anyone's decision. The safe approach is to be Switzerland—neutral. Nobody hates you. Nobody loves you. The decision to buy your home will be based on something other than the paint color."

What I Didn't Realize at the Time

The beige situation doesn't apply just to interior decorating. I recall being in the boardroom of a major law firm. We were working on a very complicated, multi-million-dollar plan to completely revamp the firm's executive and partner compensation plan (discussed in detail in the fifth secret). In an office where almost all the men wore black or navy suits, I was wearing a light-colored patterned sport coat and a pink shirt. One of the partners cleverly teased me, asking, "Do they sell men's clothes where you bought that outfit?" A female executive named Talia said, "You should talk, Frank. At least he has some style—unlike the rest of you boring old men."

I am in no position to offer fashion advice to anyone, but that is not the point of this story. The fact that I dressed differently generated some feeling, some thoughts, and even some action. I appreciated Frank's clever ball-busting and equally appreciated Talia's support. If I had worn a navy blue suit and white shirt, there would have been no commentary about my clothing and no opportunity for Talia to (directly) rag on Frank and (indirectly) on the rest of the old guard running the firm. Whether that "ice breaking" interaction contributed to what turned out to be a very successful outcome for my firm will never be known.

Interestingly, I did receive a very valuable piece of information after we beat out firms ten and 20 times our size for the very lucrative project. The law firm (correctly) assumed that we would be more flexible in our planning and delivery than the larger firms. They were more interested in our pitch of "innovation, not overhead," and were willing to work with us to find an efficient way to handle the administration. My wearing something a little different didn't close the deal, but it was consistent with the more original solution that we were offering to build. Incidentally, the representatives from the other firms who pitched before and after I did were in blue or gray suits—and all were wearing white shirts and striped ties.

"What does color have to do with my business or my financial success?"

Earlier in the book, you learned that only one in 100 families is in that 1% that controls the wealth in this country. This epiphany is right up there with the discovery that there are actually 500 companies in the Fortune 500. You also learned that a small percentage of that group earns millions of dollars per year.

If you want to achieve those levels of success, you need to become what we mathematicians refer to as an outlier. The scientific definition is "a value that lies outside [is much smaller or larger than] most of the other values in a set of data."

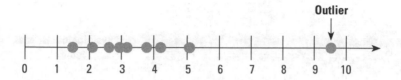

This mathematical or scientific term has taken on a slightly different meaning when talking about people or groups of people (like companies). In those cases:

Outlier (noun):
- a person or thing *differing* from the main body or system, or
- a person or thing *differing* from all other members of a particular group or set.

If you want to be unlike most of the people in this country, you need to look at things differently. You need to do things differently. Most important, you need to be different. The first step to being different is to *stop trying to fit in*! This means that you shouldn't try to fit in with the Joneses, unless you are talking about Jerry Jones (the billionaire owner of the most valuable franchise in American professional sports, the Dallas Cowboys. He has undoubtedly achieved his significant level of financial success by marching to the beat of his own drum).

Successful People Are Psychotic

I confess. This subheading demonstrates an extremely liberal interpretation of Maslow's hierarchy of needs. What I wanted to say,

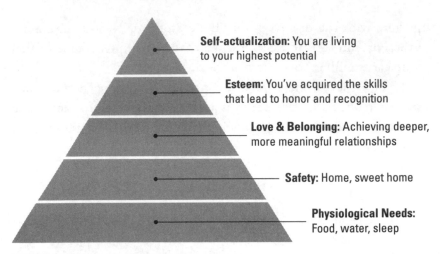

FIGURE 1: Maslow's Hierarchy

but couldn't find an impactful and truthful way to say it in a subheading, was that humans are not psychologically equipped to pursue the higher levels of success. Abraham Maslow's hierarchy of needs came from his 1943 paper, "A Theory of Human Motivation," which was published in *Psychological Review*. With apologies to Maslow, we will simplify what human beings value, in order of importance:

1. **Human survival:** air, water, food, clothing, and shelter
2. **Safety and security:** personal security, financial security, health, and well-being
3. **Social belonging:** friendships, intimacy, and family
4. **Esteem:** self-esteem and self-respect
5. **Self-actualization:** actually, too deep for this book
6. **Self-transcendence:** transcends my ability to explain

If most people want to be more successful than they are, there must be more than just the statistical explanation that only 1% of the people can be in the top 1%. As a mathematician, I can't believe that I just wrote that. But as a financial consultant for so many brilliant and motivated people, I know for a fact that psychology trumps economics when people make difficult financial decisions. For example, many people skip prenuptial planning even though the odds of a child's losing an inheritance in divorce are so great. The parents would rather not fight with their children about the prenuptial agreement than protect them from divorce (a better plan is offered in the sixth secret). I also know that money is almost always an emotional topic when you are doing financial planning. Some people fear that leaving the money to the kids may cause them to hurt themselves. Others fear that doing estate planning may cause them to die prematurely (honestly, that is a concern for many).

If you believe in Maslow's hierarchy of needs, then the feeling of social belonging is right up there with love. People don't want to be alone—literally or figuratively. The only things more important to us are our physiological needs—like air, water, food—and our need for safety. I am guessing that you could make a case that success leads to financial safety, but I am not sure that millions of years of evolution would support the purchase of a private airplane or courtside season tickets to calm a "fight or flight" reaction.

Most of us want to achieve success for some sort of esteem. Whether you are looking for someone else's approval or admiration, or working on building your own self-esteem, Maslow still has belonging ahead of esteem. What does this mean to all of us who are striving for higher levels of success? Consider what you have already learned in the last section.

Success Favors Innovators, Not Followers

You understand that the most successful are outliers in the truest sense of the word. To achieve levels of success that only one in 1,000 people do, you must be truly special. Special means that you are unlike others in some remarkable way. How are the most successful special? They are special because they do things differently. What is more interesting than *what* they do differently is *how* they are able to do things *so* differently.

The most successful have become that way because they defy the rules of psychology. The most successful didn't care what people thought about their innovative ideas. They may have looked pretty silly at times. They may have been laughed at by their former partners, their competitors, their bankers, or even their old friends. Their gracefulness (or blissful ignorance) allowed them to continue their journey toward success—even when they didn't fit in with everyone else.

Think about how crazy a thought this is. We were all once children, and then adolescents, trying desperately to fit in. If you ever heard your parents ask you, "If Johnny jumped off a bridge, would you jump after him?" or "If Mary told you to light yourself on fire, would you?" then you understand peer pressure. If you can't remember that far back, look at your children. What did they do, or what are they doing now, to try to belong in the "in" crowd? It is only human nature, but that doesn't make it any less frustrating to watch.

Unfortunately, adolescence doesn't mean the end of this driving factor. As we got older, we tried to find the right groups in college. In our first jobs, we wanted to toe the company line. We may have blindly accepted the track necessary to become partner. All states have laws that govern our behavior. Most religions have commandments, rules, or other condoned and forbidden activities. Most people avoid actions they fear their friends and relatives would criticize. At the very least, most people refrain from sharing details of their potentially unpopular activities with their family and friends. I am not implying that all Americans are sheep. Rather, I am saying that society typically rewards those who fit in with the crowd and creates more challenges for those who do not. The Pulitzer Prize-winning journalist Herbert Bayard Swope once offered, "I can't give you a sure-fire formula for success, but I can give you a formula for failure: try to please everybody all the time."

This is far from an astute observation from an armchair psychologist. It merely supports the fact that being very successful is not only mathematically difficult (with only one in 1,000 people being in the top 0.1% of earners). Maslow's hierarchy explains why it goes against the laws of psychology and human development to do the things that help people achieve the highest levels of success. You might even say that to be successful, you have to "hack" your own brain … and 200,000 years of evolution.

I am not suggesting that your instincts are 100% wrong. You wouldn't have any success already if you hadn't done something remarkably right. I am suggesting that you reverse your current detrimental attitude and behavior. I want you to go back to what helped you achieve success in the first place. Let me explain the dangerous trap that snares many successful entrepreneurs.

Get Back to Basics

When you reach a certain level of success, there is a natural tendency to try to protect what you have achieved. This is the biggest problem I see in working with successful families and businesses. Most successful people are aware that they have already beaten the odds and made more money than 99% of Americans. But instead of continuing with the type of thinking that helped them get to this level, they change their philosophy and start to focus on staying there.

You may have heard the sports concept of "playing not to lose." This is the "prevent defense" in football or the old "four corners" in basketball. Basically, when some teams get a lead in some type of timed sporting event, they stop doing what gave them the lead in the first place and start focusing on the clock. Instead of continuing to focus on what made them successful, they spend their energy waiting and hoping that everything will end in their favor. They go from being aggressive initiators to becoming very passive defenders. The result is predictable, as 70% of family businesses fail to get passed to the second generation, and 95% fail to get passed to the third generation.

As soon as you start worrying about protecting what you've built, you are turning the corner away from innovation and making your way toward standardization. Those who reach the higher levels of success never abandon the idea that they must continue to innovate. They see the world in high-definition hues. They do not worry about upsetting others and simply settle on beige.

Be George Costanza: Do the Opposite

If you are looking for an example of how to do things differently, the most entertaining example I can offer comes from the hit television show *Seinfeld*. In the 86th episode, "The Opposite," George Costanza comes back from the beach and decides that every decision he has made in his life has been wrong, and his life is the exact opposite of what it should be. Jerry convinces him that "if every instinct you have is wrong, then the opposite would have to be right."

George then introduces himself to a beautiful woman, saying, "My name is George. I'm unemployed and I live with my parents." To his surprise, she is impressed and agrees to date him. She then gets George an interview with New York Yankees owner George Steinbrenner. Instead of following his instincts and kissing Steinbrenner's ass, George boldly criticizes many of Steinbrenner's management practices. Steinbrenner is impressed with his confidence and gives George a job.

It is interesting, but not shocking, that the most successful of my company's clients have that self-esteem need met already. It manifests itself in the roles and responsibilities they give their advisors. They don't want to be surrounded with yes-men or yes-women. They want to hire the smartest and most creative advisors to question them, challenge them, and help them consider all possible, and a few impossible, solutions to a problem. In the fifth secret, I will share how the most successful not only recruit the right team of advisors, but also set up the circumstances for all of them to work best for the business or the family.

Now it's your turn. Here are a few "opposite" ideas for your consideration. You may want to rethink how you communicate your goals, where you turn for advice, how you structure relationships with advisors, and where you get your new ideas.

To reach the highest levels of success, you need to be comfortable being different. You need to accept that your outlook on money, business, and success will differ from that of your friends and family. If your only comfort comes from doing something and knowing that everyone else is doing it too, then you either have to replace all of your friends with people who are far more successful than you are, or you have to accept that fact that you will struggle mightily to achieve anything more than moderate success.

Before you can be truly comfortable being different from others around you, you must know who you really are. When you get to that level of acceptance, people will describe you as being "comfortable in your own skin." For me, this took a very long time. I took every personality test under the sun, worked with therapists, and did countless mediations on finding my purpose. Though the journey can be long, the rewards are extraordinary. Being comfortable with being different was the key to my success—and it will be one significant key to yours.

How does being different apply to financial success? In social circles, you won't let other people's fears and worries hold you back. You know you will take chances, experience setbacks, and live to fight another day (covered in the third secret). When working with professionals, you will resist the urge to accept "off the rack" solutions and financial products. You know that millions of advisors can offer fast and easy answers, but that is neither what you want nor what you need. The most successful embrace the fact that their unique financial, legal, and tax challenges will require paying innovative advisors to come up with custom solutions.

The wealthiest families don't pay attention to television, radio, or social media advertising. They know the marketing propaganda was developed for tens of millions of potential buyers. Any product or service that is appropriate for tens of millions of people is not part of anyone's innovative strategy—except the company that is trying to find a way to sell its wares to tens of millions of people. This will be covered in greater detail in the fifth secret.

Don't Believe What You Read

Most successful people are curious. They value education greatly. They are constantly striving to find better ways to manage or grow their wealth. They want to explore new ideas in hopes of finding something that may be useful to them. It's not uncommon to look for bits of inexpensive advice on websites, in magazines and newspapers, and on television or radio programs. If people didn't rely on recommendations that come in a popular magazine or on a free website directed to millions of average people, there wouldn't be any advertising in those periodicals or on those sites.

Though the information in the popular press may be presented in an interesting fashion, it is unlikely to be useful for people with very ambitious financial goals. The most successful never give a second thought to any financial or legal suggestion that is offered by someone who isn't intimately familiar with their situation and goals. They don't *want* to spend the time and money on customized planning—they know that they *must* spend the time and money on a specially trained and highly experienced team of advisors to customize a plan that will help them most efficiently and effectively reach their specific, personal goals. It is because of their elevated perspective, willingness to look very different from everyone else, and gracefulness that I refer to these successful pioneers as "giraffes."

Bigger Corporations Have Bigger Problems and Worse Options

The same problems we are discussing regarding individuals and family businesses are present in larger corporations. I recently had lunch with a friend of mine who is the general counsel for a publicly traded bank. He said the bank never stops talking about trying to be innovative in its commodity industry—which is no easy feat.

He said that the bank just spent (wasted?) millions of dollars in consulting fees paid to Boston Consulting Group (BCG) to get suggestions for innovation. I know some very intelligent people who have worked for BCG and the other strategy consulting firms (McKinsey & Company and Bain & Company are two that come to mind). These firms have many more attorneys on staff than I do, so I am always quick to point out that they do very good work. Management consulting is a huge industry. In 2016, it was a $71.2 billion industry, with more than 600,000 employees. Many of these employees have advanced degrees from some of the most prestigious universities in the world. See Table 7.

TABLE 7: Number of Employees Working for Large Strategy Consulting Firms*

Accenture	394,000
Bain & Company	7,000
Boston Consulting Group	6,200
Booz Allen Hamilton	22,000
Deloitte	244,400
EY (formerly Ernst & Young)	231,000
KPMG	188,000
McKinsey & Company	14,400
PricewaterhouseCoopers	223,000

*Not all employees work in management or strategy consulting.

If you have a service firm with thousands of employees, you undoubtedly have defined systems, processes, and controls in place. This allows you to manage a large organization with multiple offices, projects, and employees working in many states and countries. To leverage the size and infrastructure of such an organization, you must standardize the data collection, analyses, and presentations so that thousands of people can understand their roles without having to redefine them, and relearn them, for each project. Big firms with big reputations must protect their brands and their profitability. How well each firm balances normalizing the engagement process to maximize the value to the consulting firm with innovating for the benefit of the client will ultimately be decided by each client... after the fact.

Here is the question that I'd like to ask the CEO of a publicly traded company: "Do you think it is efficient and cost-effective for a company with 7,000 employees to hire another firm with 6,000 or 14,000 or 200,000 employees to help you with your innovation challenges?"

I also want to ask, "Do you think you will get innovative ideas from a company that works with dozens of firms in your same industry, or do you think you will get much of the same advice it has already given your competitors?" You should ask yourself, "Do I think that these large consulting operations see themselves as integral parts of my long-term mission, or are they more likely to see me as a source of recurring revenues that will fuel theirs?"

Are you hiring this firm to give you the unicorn of an idea that will separate you from your competition? Does its deliverable have you seeing a rainbow of opportunities, or is it just giving you a slightly different shade of beige than what it gave your competition last year?

Timing Is Everything

Doing something differently helps you stand out in a crowd. I am not saying that you always want to stick out. There are a time and a place for everything. Mark Twain is credited with saying, "Comedy is tragedy plus time." This is likely the genesis of a famous line used by comedian Jeff Ross. Ross is often called "The RoastMaster General" because of his cleverly demeaning comments about celebrities and public figures that take place during roasts. Whenever he says something that elicits a groan from the crowd, he will stop and ask, "Too soon?"

Think about this concept with respect to your financial decisions. Most people don't seriously consider applying for insurance until after a loss occurs. Most investors are tempted to get out of the market after they lose money. Most people consider estate planning and business succession after someone passes away. Most companies don't rethink their executive benefits and retention planning until after they lose someone very valuable to the organization. Most businesses don't address corporate governance until after they get into some serious trouble. Lastly, and most important, most corporations completely ignore the need for innovation until after a new competitor enters the market and rocks their world. All too often, it's too little and it's too late. There is a real example going on as I write this. People in Houston are all much more interested in flood insurance today, a week after Hurricane Harvey displaced a huge part of the Gulf of Mexico into the city.

I understand that many of you are thinking that you will just wait until there is a "better time" to take action. You have a mortgage (or two), young kids, clients, and other obligations. You can wait for a better time to adjust your goals, fix your business, or pursue your dreams. Having done this numerous times, I can tell you that the better time is never going to come. Your young kids will grow older and need to be shuttled around. Shortly after they learn to drive and don't require your parental taxi service, they will be off to college—creating a much larger financial obligation for you. Your business will only become more complicated. The number of employees you have will likely continue to grow. The debts and mortgages will likely increase as your success grows. If you don't take massive action soon, you never will. Now is the time for you to act on these goals.

See a Better Path

If it were left to luck, being very successful would be almost impossible. When you consider that the human psyche is designed to steer us clear of the activities that lead to maximum success, it's no wonder that people don't reach their goals.

The most successful entrepreneurs, families, and executives have taught us that the journey of a pioneer is often a very lonely one. You should now appreciate that the road to great success will never be crowded. When you try to do the impossible, you can expect no shortage of people telling you that your ideas are unreasonable, imprudent, or downright stupid.

You now accept the fact that, as a pioneer, you must walk where nobody ever has. You must do things that others have not succeeded in doing. You know that there certainly will not be anybody on the other side to congratulate you for properly following the path. There was no path!

Later in the book, you will learn how to create conditions where your employees, partners, investors, and advisors are all on the same page with you. These arrangements will be of great importance for you to feel that sense of belonging, even as you are doing something unique and disruptive. This sense of belonging will help you overcome the psychological challenges that Maslow pointed out almost 75 years ago.

You should accept the challenge. You can reach your ambitious goals. You will learn better ways to get there by reading the rest of the book. You are on your way.

Exercise: You may already be very clear about your goals for success. If so, please continue reading. If you are not clear about your goals, or you are sufficiently motivated to set more ambitious goals for yourself, it is a great time for you to go to the "Setting *Your* Ambitious Goals" section mentioned in the Additional Resources at the end of this book and available at www.JarvisTower.com/resources.

CHAPTER 4

The Second Secret: *More* Is More— Maximize Your Leverage

You have already learned the first secret—Stop Being Beige. If you want to achieve the highest levels of success, you must have *your own* clear definition of success. You must be careful not to get your advice from people who are not in the economic class that you wish to reach. You should try not to worry about popular opinion, because you are looking to achieve success that very few will ever realize.

Hopefully, with your newly found appreciation and motivation, you will take some time to complete the exercises mentioned in the Additional Resources. You may prefer to read book all the way through, then go back to the exercises, or you may prefer to do them before going any further. The key is to go back to the text after you have defined what success means to you. This will allow you to apply the secrets of the most successful to your particular goal. You'll learn from the exercises (or have already learned) that success cannot be defined by just a list of what you want to accomplish financially. Your definition of success should have all five of these elements:

> *"Success is doing what you want,*
> *where you want,*
> *when you want,*
> *with whom you want,*
> *as much as you want."* —TONY ROBBINS

If you came up with a goal that has these elements, you now have a clear vision of how much you want to earn or accomplish in your lifetime. More important, you have a road map for *how* you want to get there. You know where you want to be living and working, what role *you* want to be playing, who is going to be working with you, and to whom you will be providing your special products or services. You may also know how much time you will dedicate to this endeavor so you have enough time for the other important things in your life.

Developing this clear vision of what you want your life to look and feel like is of the utmost importance. Setting and achieving significant goals is the only way to have a truly fulfilling life. You have accomplished Step 1—setting the goal. However, it is only the beginning. Dreaming of reaching a goal will get you only so far. You need a plan, and you will need to execute that plan if you are to turn your dreams into reality.

Hopefully, you set a big goal—a really big goal—for yourself, your company, or your family. The bigger the goal, the more obstacles you will have to overcome. The greater the number of obstacles, the more detailed your execution plan will have to be for you to arrive in the promised land.

Before you curse me for suggesting adding dozens, if not hundreds, of items to your already seemingly unattainable to-do list, you need to know something about me. I hate lists. Like many mathematicians, I have a very well-developed "right brain." I am ultra-creative, highly strategic, a complete non-conformist. Some might go so far as to call me an anarchist, but they don't have the authority to make such a claim. I have also been diagnosed with attention deficit disorder (ADD), so the probability that I would get bored with any long-drawn-out process is high.

You may question that diagnosis because I have written 14 books. What you don't know is that I usually procrastinate for six months, then write the entire book in two to four weeks. To steal a line from a self-help guru I admire: I don't say that to impress you; I say it to impress upon you that I really hate adding anything to my procrastination list—I mean, to-do list.

Because of my personal disdain for long processes and routine and because I am doing the writing, I will take the liberty of projecting those same preferences onto you. As an entrepreneur, I have lots of new ideas that capture (and divert) my attention. I like to explore new ideas and take on new challenges. I have no interest in solving the same problem twice. This is why my firm, JarvisTower, doesn't handle basic financial, economic, or business consulting. Literally, we tell people that we focus on "wacky institutional shit"—the wackier, the better.

I share this information about me so that you understand my biases. Because of my biases, I am going to assume that you want to undertake only the challenges that will give you immediate and significant results. I also presume that you want suggestions that you will not have to regularly monitor, review, or manage. Lastly, I assume that you would much rather pursue your wacky ideas than manage someone else's labor-intensive system for success. With apologies to Clyde Frazier (the former New York Knicks' great and masterful play-by-play announcer), with those aforementioned assumptions and presumptions, I will say with great gumption that the rest of this book is designed for your consumption. Or, translated from Frazier-ese to English, my goal is to give you the tools to free up as much time and money as possible to help you get to as many of your ideas as possible—provided that is part of your definition of success.

I admit that there is a sense of accomplishment that washes over me after toiling on a project and ultimately grinding something out. I bet that you have done more than your fair share of "grinding out" over the years. My guess is that you picked up this book because you were tired of grinding out your successes and you were looking for a better path. You have come to the right place. This is exactly what we are going to help you understand and implement.

You now have this huge goal of changing your business and your approach to wealth. You are going to make big changes so that you can achieve a new level of success while actually enjoying more of your life, and the people in it, along the way. This is a big shift, and it will be worth the effort. The goal of this book is to help you speed up your process so that you can get there faster, more cheaply, and with less aggravation.

The way to accomplish all of this is with one thing: **leverage.**

What Is Leverage?

Google the word "leverage." You'll see links to websites for the Cambridge English dictionary, Merriam-Webster dictionary, Investopedia, and to thesauraus.com. You will find definitions of "leverage" as a noun and a verb. You will find both financial and business definitions.

Google offers four definitions of "leverage." Here's one:

lev·er·age *verb*: 2. use (something) to maximum advantage.
"the organization needs to leverage its key resources"

Thesaurus.com offers a list of synonyms. I am partial to these four:

1. Influence
2. Advantage
3. Edge
4. Power

If you can influence others to help you gain an advantage or an edge over your competition, you will have successfully achieved some level of power.

You will even find technical and mechanical definitions that are rather inspirational—as you may want to see how much force you can exert on a screwdriver to your temple after reading them. One comprehensive, if not screwdriver-worthy, definition of leverage comes from BusinessDictionary.com:

The ability to influence a system, or an environment, in a way that multiplies the outcome of one's efforts without a corresponding increase in the consumption of resources. In other words, leverage is the advantageous condition of having a relatively small amount of cost yield a relatively high level of returns.

Leverage allows a person to be more efficient, more effective, and much more powerful. Leverage helps you get more done in less time, with less effort, and with less money. Do you know anyone who wants to spend more time and money while working even harder? If you are looking for a shortcut to financial success, leverage is the better path.

The Importance of Leverage

Earlier, you learned the differences between the middle-to-upper classes of Americans and the group we refer to as the successful—the higher earners who have built significantly more wealth and influence than their peers. The successful know that leverage is the single most important tool to building wealth. Without leverage, they would have to do everything themselves. They would have to run their own businesses and handle all of their financial affairs. They would pay for everything with only their own money and would micro-manage the hell out of everything at work and at home. With those constraints, businesses and personal wealth would grow organically—at a snail's pace. If you resemble this remark, then you have not yet embraced the importance of leverage.

You can use leverage to make your life easier. You can use leverage to "buy time." By being more efficient, you will free yourself to do those things you identified in the first secret as being most important to you. Whether your current goal is maximizing your profitability, increasing enterprise value so you can sell your company, or finding time for the most enjoyable elements of life, leverage is your passport to Successville. Let's look at specific applications of leverage that I have learned from my most successful clients and colleagues.

Leverage Limitations

If some leverage is good, more leverage is better. Who wouldn't want to get more done with less effort or less money? The successful have tried to maximize leverage for thousands of years. It may seem like the amount of leverage one can attain is endless, but there are some rules that just can't be broken (not even by the most disruptive of us). Consider the following:

1. You have only so much energy.
2. You have only 24 hours in a day.
3. You have only so much money.
4. You can borrow only so much money.
5. You can manage only so many people.

When you reach the safe limits for each of these variables, you have reached your maximum capacity. Efficiency is achieved when leverage is increased to a point where you have approached your capacity without exceeding it.

It is important not to exceed your capacity. When you push too hard, something is going to break. Your health, your marriage, or your relationship with your bank may suffer. When something important breaks, you have to start all over again. Duplication of effort is not a sign of efficiency. Having to go back to the start and retrace multiple steps is the opposite of using leverage. It will severely deter your progress, if not derail you completely.

The key is to maximize leverage without exceeding your capacity and creating a catastrophic disaster. The third secret will show you many ways to protect yourself from the mistakes that you might otherwise make, but that is not a license to work yourself to death by pushing too hard. Leverage is about working smarter, not harder. For this reason, increasing effort is not using leverage at all. Getting better results from less effort is the best way to achieve extraordinary levels of success.

Financial Leverage

You understand that leverage is the key to working smarter, not harder. You also learned that having money definitely helps you make more money. When you combine those two concepts, you get financial leverage. These applications can help you pull more levers to help you achieve the highest levels of success.

Think about the most amazing sites you have ever seen. Which was most impressive? Was it the Coliseum in Rome, the pyramids of Giza, or possibly the Great Wall of China? Maybe it was one of the two tallest buildings in the world: Burj Khalifa in Dubai or the Shanghai Tower. It's okay if you were most impressed with Mall of the Americas. In these building projects, levers were used in the construction. Whether the builders used an ancient pulley system to construct the pyramids or a modern system of cranes to construct a half-mile-tall building, the most spectacular construction projects all required innovative uses of leverage.

Financial endeavors are similar to construction projects. The more ambitious the goal, the greater the need for creative blueprints. That is only the beginning, as many people are needed to carry out the plans. In construction, there are a general contractor and scores of subcontractors. Financial planning is similar to construction in many ways. Someone has to be the architect of the plan that meets the client's goals and desires. Multiple specialists need to deliver expertise along the way. Somebody needs to oversee the process and make sure all the parts are working smoothly together. Unfortunately, working smoothly is much more the exception than the rule.

In working with thousands of professionals over the last 20-plus years, I have learned the single biggest difference between the planning for the most successful clients and the planning for others. Most people work on their wealth part-time—when they aren't working in their businesses. The most successful prioritize their wealth, and they hire extraordinary talent. They pay them to run things by each other too. This is going to be covered in the fifth secret, but it is important to review it here so you keep this in mind as you continue through the book.

Without exception, every multi-million-dollar earner and every $50 million family I know focuses on financial leverage as a key to success. Let's look at some specific ways to do this.

Types of Financial Leverage

Financial leverage can be accomplished by leveraging the two most important resources: time and money. When we talk about leveraging time, we are talking about limiting the amount of effort we must exert or patience we must have.

Buying Time

In previous books, I used to call this concept "leveraging effort." I probably wrote that when I was in my 20s and pretty lazy. I thought the key was to get other people to do things for me. Though that concept is important (and covered in the fifth secret), it is not nearly as important as saving time. There are many things we would all do *if we only had more hours in the day.* This is why leveraging time is integral to your success.

Consider how you acted when you were young. You may not have truly believed that you were immortal, but your behavior indicated otherwise. I remember college like it was yesterday, though my 25-year reunion is later this year. We all remember driving fast, looking for all-you-can-eat buffets, and drinking cheap beer. Inexplicably, most of us bought the cheapest toilet paper because those precious few moments each day weren't worth the extra three cents. Hell, we even thought pre-paying for a five-night stay in Las Vegas for the slightly lower rate was a great idea.

As we all grew older, we gained that all-too-valuable elevated perspective. I turned 47 while writing this book. I know 47 is not that old, but I am closer to 70 than I am to my college graduation. That sucks. But with age does come experience. We start to accept that we have less time. We need to make smart choices—about our time, our friends, and our health. When you have less time, you naturally become less patient. If you are unsure of that one, ask yourself if you have ever wondered, "Why does the microwave take so long to heat up this food?"

Still not convinced that impatience is setting in for you? Have you ever been on vacation, with no agenda, and felt agitated by the slow service? It's not only slow food service that bugs us. We now have less patience for ignorance and stupidity. We have less patience for technology. We have less patience for everything—including financial success. Consider this experience I had.

Education at 30,000 Feet

I once sat next to a senior executive from GE Capital (the financial services unit of General Electric). The man was in charge of healthcare acquisitions. At the time, I had just released my fifth book for physicians, and I was helping a couple of my doctor clients sell their patents and businesses. I remember what this man told me about GE's strategy for investing in (buying) businesses. He told me that the largest company in the world was not buying technology. It had the resources to figure out anything it wanted to figure out—including how to get around any patents people might have. When GE wrote a check, it was buying time! By purchasing the technology, it was saving itself years of research and development so it could get something to market before someone else did. This conversation left such an impression upon me that I am writing about it 12 years later.

This is a valuable lesson for all of you smarty-pants types out there. You can have an IQ of 140 or 150 or even 160. I am not saying that you are not as smart, or smarter, than some of the other people who are out there offering you advice. I am saying that you have only so much time. That time may be best utilized closing the next deal, developing the next technology, or finding the next strategic partner. There is power in "smart partnering" with other people so that you can save yourself the time needed to do it yourself. In the fourth and fifth secrets, you will learn how to get advisors in the insurance, investment, accounting, and legal professions to work with you, instead of for you (or against you, as many of you claim they do). When you structure the relationships and the engagements properly, you will save valuable time and effort—and all of these things will lead to making more money. This is the next sub-category of leverage.

Making Money Work for You

Nothing is free. There's some sage wisdom for you right there. Seriously, every client I have ever had has always wished he or she had more money. I am not suggesting that any of these people are greedy by any means. It is not uncommon for an executive making $1 million per year to balk at the buyout price of a competitor or to hesitate to hire a superstar CFO who might cost 40% more than an average executive.

Even the two billionaires who have hired me recently have expressed that they have cash flow challenges. One was heavily invested in real estate. He had lots of leverage that was restricting the family's ability to pursue some new ventures. The other was trying to build a foundation that would change the face of education in this country. They had cash flow challenges hindering everything that they wanted to do. I am not asking for violin players to step up and play a sad song for them. I am merely pointing out that we all have dreams that we don't have the resources to fund.

This is definitely the case with wealth. I refer to it here as making money, but it could easily be called leveraging resources, since wealth can be cash, securities, land, or business interests. In a world of commodity products like securities, real estate, loans, legal documents, and insurance, you would expect these products to be highly efficient. In the upper end of town, where the clients are very busy and very successful, the service industries have managed to find a way to preserve significant fees and expenses in the products and services they offer. If you can save some of these fees and still receive extraordinary service, you can use that "found" money to fuel some of your expansion plans or to fund your new ventures. These will be discussed throughout, but they are the focus of the fourth and fifth secrets.

Leveraging Time and Money: The Power of People

When you leverage people, you can actually save yourself time and money. The most successful know that leveraging the efforts of other people is one way to get more than 24 hours of work done in a day. By leveraging people with special skills and expertise you don't possess, you can save yourself valuable time. By hiring lawyers, you get to skip three *years* of law school. We all go to see the doctor because we don't want to spend seven-plus years in training and hundreds of thousands of dollars to be able to treat ourselves. But beware: leveraging people is a double-edged sword.

When you leverage other people to do certain tasks, you lose control of the process. If you don't hire the right people, or put them into a structure that affords you the optimal amount of control and access, you may not get the outcome you want. In the fourth and fifth secrets, you will learn how to structure entities that will help align your goals and desires with those valuable people you will need to bring on board to achieve the leverage you require.

Leveraging Time (Effort)

Hard work is one key to success. You and I both know this from our own experiences. I try to explain it to my kids all the time—but they were never hungry a day in their lives, literally or figuratively. I fear this is one of those life lessons they will just have to learn on their own.

Have you ever heard the phrase, "If you want to find a faster way to get a job done, give it to the laziest man?" The goal of this chapter on leverage is to help you get the most out of any level of effort. Whether you fancy yourself hardworking or lazy, leverage can help you get more out of your desired amount of effort.

In this chapter, we will discuss the capacity problems of leverage and how education can increase your ability to leverage your effort, and then I'll offer ways that the most successful overcome the barriers of capacity.

Save the Hard-Work Talk for Your Kids

The basic and inherent problem with effort is that you have only two hands and there are only 24 hours in a day. Let's consider the case of two fishermen, Slack Jack and Fresh Fred, with very different work ethics, to illustrate these constraints.

■ **CASE STUDY**

Go Fish—Slack Jack and Fresh Fred

Let's assume that Slack Jack and Fresh Fred earn $5 per pound of fish they bring in each week. Slack Jack works five days per week. He fishes for five hours per day and catches 20 pounds of fish per hour. If he brings in 100 pounds of fish per day, he will earn $2,500 per week before paying overhead, his first mate, equipment, taxes, and so forth.

Fresh Fred works six days per week and fishes for seven hours every day. He also catches 20 pounds of fish per hour. This gives Fred little time off for family or hobbies, but he does earn $8,400 per week before all his expenses—which are considerably higher than Jack's because the first mate, gasoline, and bait aren't free.

Both of these fishermen might consider themselves successful (depending on their goals and values). But if hardworking Fresh Fred wants to make more money, there aren't enough hours in the day or days in the week for him to make any more money unless he does something that earns him more money per hour or he finds a way to leverage something other than his own effort. Other applications of leverage could help him do just that.

Leveraging Education

The idea of leveraging education to create wealth is no secret. In fact, it has become part of the American Dream. For more than a century, immigrants have come to the US and taken advantage of the educational system. They have pushed their children to do well in school in the hope that the children would get good jobs and enjoy higher standards of living. They have also pushed their children to find careers that pay them more money than Fresh Fred. This was eloquently and emotionally illustrated in Ramon Peralta's 2017 commencement speech to the University of Bridgeport's graduating class.

Leveraging education is a key element of fortune building and maintaining wealth. To prove this point, let's consider some salaries of highly educated people. When considering the earning potential in these professions, keep in mind that the median household income (including the outliers) is approximately $62,000. This means that half of all United States households earn less than $62,000 per year. What does education offer?

- The first-year salary plus signing bonus for an MBA (2 years of graduate school) is $135,000 (www.managementconsulted.com).

- The median annual salary for a neurosurgeon in the US was $548,186 in 2013 (www.ehow.com).

Neurosurgery requires completion of four years of medical school and then a one-year internship and a rigorous five to seven years of residency. You can see that leveraging education can help you earn more money per year and increase your wealth faster than if you have a job that requires a lower level of education, no matter how hard you work.

Education and Effort Are Not Enough

Would you be surprised to hear that a neurosurgeon and Larry the Landscaper have the same problem? While we are not saying that Larry is performing brain surgery, we are suggesting that they both have the same fundamental problem—albeit at different levels of income. Larry doesn't have enough hours in the day or days in the week to increase his business. Similarly, a neurosurgeon's income is limited by the number of surgeries he can perform, which is also limited by the number of hours in a day and days in a week.

Even if you assume that there are an endless supply of patients who need brain surgery and an endless supply of lawns to be mowed, both the landscaper earning $50 per hour and the neurosurgeon earning $500 per hour have the same capacity problem, because:

1. They are limited in the amount of money they can earn until they figure out how to leverage what they do.
2. They make money only when they are actually working.

This is a lesson that the most successful figured out long ago. The secret to long-term success is leverage. The keys to using leverage correctly are:

1. Always focus on possible points of leverage in any business
2. Never consider increasing effort as a legitimate, long-term means to growth
3. Never enter into a business that requires you to be involved in day-to-day operations.

For these reasons, at JarvisTower we prefer to focus our articles, seminars, books, and personal consulting recommendations on strategies that help leverage assets *and* leverage people.

Leveraging Resources

You remember the phrase "It takes money to make money" that was discussed in chapter 2. The economic data supports the claim that having lots of disposable income definitely contributes to exponential wealth accumulation. There are other valuable resources, beyond your money, that you will want to leverage. You will now learn how to leverage:

1. Your own money
2. Other people's money (sometimes shortened to OPM)
3. Intellectual property

Leveraging Your Own Money

Leveraging your own money is the oldest and most basic form of leverage. It has been documented all the way back to ancient times, involving nations, empires, kings, and emperors. These nations had enough money to fund expeditions to discover new lands and acquire even more wealth. You can see the spoils of war on a visit to any of the museums in Rome, to the Tower of London, or to the more recently unearthed tomb of Liu Fei in Jiangsu, China.

Today, you can witness similar leveraging right here in the US. The successful make their capital work for them in various ways. If you have money, you can purchase land or real estate and lease it to others who can't afford to buy the property outright. If you have excess money you don't need to spend to support your lifestyle, you can put it into long-term investments that have higher expected returns than shorter-term investments. These may be investments that are unavailable to investors who require a short-term return to pay bills. Lastly, when you have money, you can use it as collateral to borrow money and use other's people money to make money, too. This is what the successful do all the time to maximize wealth. This is the next application of leverage.

Leveraging Other People's Money

Generally, using other people's money is considered the classic type of leverage. Using OPM as leverage often refers to credit, but we will broaden it to include all types of leverage involving OPM.

The most common way to use OPM is through debt. Many families have achieved their wealth by borrowing at lower rates and investing the loan proceeds to achieve greater returns. This is a common practice among real estate investors. They put down a small percentage of the total costs to build properties and use OPM to fund the remainder of the costs. By borrowing money from the bank at rates that may be as low as 6% to 8% and developing properties that may have an overall return of 15% per year, the investors use leverage to gain a significant return on his or her investment. Consider the following:

TABLE 8: Financial Leverage in Real Estate Transactions

Investor	Amount invested	Rate	Amount earned
Bank + Developer	$10 million	15%	$1,150,000
Bank	$8 million	8%	$640,000
Developer	$2 million	25%	$510,000

Based on these numbers, the developer can achieve a 25% return on an investment by using OPM leverage to fund a project anticipated to yield a 15% total return. This is a classic example of how leverage works with real estate.

In other situations, such as starting a business or making another speculative investment, the successful can assume higher levels of risk because they don't need the money to pay for living expenses. This allows them to take chances and realize higher investment returns than less risky investments offer.

Another way to leverage OPM is through *equity*—that is, taking someone else's money and providing a piece of a business or an investment in return. In this situation, the investor takes more risk but also gets a higher expected return than the bank would get with debt. Though this kind of deal ultimately costs the successful a larger portion of the total return, it doesn't have monthly or annual payment requirements the way a loan does. This gives the most successful greater short-term freedom with regard to cash flow, because no interest or principal payments are due. In fact, even if there is a profit, the successful American may be able to effectively borrow the investor's share simply by not distributing it and reinvesting in the next project.

Equity is best suited for deals that are more speculative and cannot guarantee regular short-term income. Even well-established, publicly traded companies such as AT&T, Disney, Oracle, and so on do this on occasion. Many wealthy Americans have learned a lesson from these companies and have offered equity positions to investors to help fund the growth of family wealth while offering participation in the upside.

Leveraging Intellectual Property

Since World War II, the most significant wealth accumulation has resulted from leveraging intellectual property. This intellectual property could be an idea, such as McDonald's fast-food assembly line concept, or the technology behind social networking sites that millions of people use, such as Facebook or Snapchat.

Other forms of intellectual property include copyrights on things like the *Star Wars* or *Harry Potter* stories. In each of these cases, an individual or a small group of partners comes up with an idea, proves it can work, legally protects the idea, and then attempts to leverage it in ways that allow them to make money as a result of other people's efforts. Let's consider three examples:

1. Bill Gates and Microsoft created the Windows operating system. Until recently, Microsoft didn't create a desktop or laptop computer to run the operating system. Instead, it created a system that other people would run on 95% of the computers in the world. Every computer that is built to run Windows results in a licensing fee paid to Microsoft. Gates didn't have to drive the increase in the sale of computers. Rather, he found a way to profit from the efforts of all the other companies that were building and selling computers, and from the efforts of all the software manufacturers that were designing products to make the use of a computer is a more enjoyable, and necessary, part of life.

2. George Lucas created the *Star Wars* concept. He made a few movies that became classics. The interest in the characters and story line didn't end with the movies. It expanded to action figures, lunch boxes, video games, and countless other items that were based on his concepts. Lucas could have tried the do-it-yourself technique, but that would have yielded only a fraction of the financial profit the leveraged approach did. Instead, he licensed his intellectual property to other people. Their efforts made Lucas hundreds of millions, if not billions, of dollars.

3. McDonald's franchises are all over the world. One successful restaurant might have generated $100,000 to $250,000 of annual profit. But this international chain of restaurants whose focus is on fast, consistently prepared food has served 3 billion customers and is worth billions.

My mother works with brothers Conrad and Mark Wetterau. They would certainly be considered part of the most successful. They own Anheuser-Busch InBev wholesalerships and a company called Golden State Foods. You may think that the food is small potatoes (pun intended) and the beer is where all the money is. Think again.

Golden State Foods is one of the largest diversified suppliers to Quick Serve Restaurant and retail industries with McDonald's as their largest worldwide customer. The $6 billion company is values-based, employing over 7,000 associates and servicing more than 125,000 restaurants from its 50 locations on 5 continents. Core businesses include processing and distribution of liquid products, meat products producer, and dairy. They also offer a variety of networked solutions for the total supply chain spectrum?

Having toured one of their facilities in southern California, I can tell you that it is an extraordinary facility with processes and controls that would blow your mind. I learned more about operations management during my one day at Golden State Foods than I learned in two years of business school. Like the rest of the McDonald's system, Golden State Foods is an operation designed to create consistency and maximize leverage.

In less extreme cases, every city has a restaurant, dry cleaner, or other business that isn't particularly profitable on an individual basis. However, the owner may be able to take a unique approach, branding, experience, or know-how and open additional locations and achieve a higher level of financial success. This is how many small-business owners attempt to use leverage. Later, we will explore how publicly traded companies get much greater leverage through public markets by buying private companies for a fraction of the value they will generate.

Leveraging People: Basic Building Blocks

While leveraging assets is fundamental to wealth building, you cannot achieve the highest levels of success without leveraging the efforts of other people. No matter how successful you are, you still have only 168 hours in your week. Every investment, each transaction, requires people to manage it. As you become more successful, you will undoubtedly experience capacity problems.

No leverage discussion would be complete without mentioning the leverage of other people's time and energy. In fact, the leverage of people is so important to your success that I have broken it up into two sections. Here, you will learn the basic benefits of leveraging employees and advisors. In the fifth secret, you will learn very advanced methods of leveraging employees by transforming employment expenses into valuable long-term assets of your organization. In the fourth and fifth secrets, you will also learn how to more creatively structure your relationships with your advisors so they work better for you and your family.

Leveraging Employees—the Basics

The most common method of leveraging people is hiring employees. Those with the financial means can afford to hire other people to do jobs for them. The employer has successfully leveraged people if the collective group of employees helps the owner earn more money than the cost of the employee salaries and benefits.

The more employees you have, the more potential leverage opportunities you have. You might hire staff to support these employees. That is an investment that you hope increases the productivity of the other employees by more than the cost of the administrative help. To leverage your employees successfully and yield an increased profit, a simple rule is to pay people less than the value they provide your firm. Law firms have practiced this method for years.

For example, law firms may charge clients $200 per hour for an attorney's services and may require the attorneys to bill 2,000 hours per year. Though the firm collects $400,000 for the services of that attorney, it might spend only $300,000 for that particular attorney's salary, benefits, and allocated overhead. The firm earns $100,000 per year for that attorney.

If the firm can afford to hire ten, 20, or 100 less experienced attorneys and can find enough work to keep them busy, the senior partners of the firm can earn a very nice living—ten to 25 times that of average Americans and five to ten times that of a less experienced attorney. By hiring less experienced attorneys, law firms are leveraging their employees very productively. They are training less expensive attorneys to do the legal work, enabling the senior partners to land lucrative contracts and build valuable relationships for the firm.

In most circumstances, an owner doesn't get to "bill out" employees. This makes it much more difficult to quantify the financial return on a leveraged person than it was in the law firm example. Often there may be equally important qualitative benefits above and beyond the quantitative ones. Consider the benefits of leveraging employees below:

- By leveraging some employees, you can spend your time performing tasks that create greater profits. This is a quantifiable benefit. Using the example above, by having associates do the work, the law firm partners (also called "rainmakers") can do what they are best at doing: bringing in new business. This is likely a much more effective use of these attorneys' time. Borrowing an idea from the bestselling book *The 4-Hour Workweek*, I want you to ask yourself, what is the best use of your time? Is it possible to pay someone to do the least profitable tasks you currently do? If so, you can take advantage of leverage.

- By leveraging an employee, you can spend your time doing things you want to do. This is an important but unquantifiable benefit. If you could have employees perform more of your work, perhaps you could spend time doing something you prefer to do, such as playing golf, spending time with family, or creating a new business that is closer to your passion. This is not financial leverage; it is emotional leverage. You can increase your quality of life by using leverage to "buy time." What can be important that that?

- By leveraging experts, you are able to "rent" other people's expertise at a reduced cost. As we will see in the fifth secret, leveraging professionals is a cost-effective way to spend your time working on profit-generating tasks and to "rent" the expertise of professional advisors. While it is possible that you could learn to become a CPA, a money manager, and an attorney, learning these jobs would not be time well spent, since you would use this knowledge only intermittently. This would take you away from things that are good uses of your time.

Leveraging people who have expertise is very economical. You can pay them less to help you than it would cost you (in time, money, and aggravation) to learn these fields yourself and then try to do the work yourself. Bill Gates didn't learn how to build computers, and George Lucas didn't learn how to make action figures; instead they both benefited from other people's expertise. Very advanced, and potentially game-changing, strategies for leveraging your employees are covered in the fifth secret. You'll learn how to increase the profitability and sale value of your company while building a team of dedicated, loyal, and hardworking employees who will act like owners!

Leveraging Advisors—the Basics

Leveraging advisors is absolutely integral to long-term financial success. Your epiphany will be when you realize that your time is worth more than your money. You should never spend your precious time on a task that could be done more efficiently and effectively by someone else. The importance of that statement is further amplified when the task in question requires special knowledge or experience. Consider the following case study:

■ **CASE STUDY**

Forget the Cobbler's Son; the Brain Surgeon Abuses His Own Brain

Nick the Neurosurgeon is massively underinsured. He has $30,000 per month of disability income insurance. His agent tells him that is all he can secure for him, even though Nick earns over $2 million per year. Nick spends night after night researching disability insurance. He learns about personal policies and group policies. He explores ways to structure multi-physician associations and legal structures to try to increase his coverage. He eventually finds out that Lloyd's of London offers policies with limits in excess of $100,000 per month. He makes call after call to Lloyd's syndicates, only to find out that he can't buy the policy directly.

Nick eventually reads one of my physician-specific financial books and calls my office. I introduce him to a friend of mine, Dan Aceti. Dan is a disability specialist who has worked on executive disability solutions with Lloyd's of London for as long as I've known him. Dan was able to help Nick navigate the confusing policy language and the long list of complicating add-ons. In the end, Dan helped Nick avoid some of the more expensive policy terms that Nick mistakenly thought he needed to purchase. Ultimately, Dan secured a $100,000-per-month disability income insurance policy for Nick.

Was this a success? Nick did get the policy he wanted, but he spent almost 40 hours researching, reading, and looking for this coverage. The equivalent of one week's work is worth about $40,000 to Nick. I am guessing that Nick would have enjoyed a week of golfing on the beach or with his kids more than he enjoyed reading about disability income policies.

Insurance is a very common area of concern in which highly educated people insist on trying to do it themselves. This is likely a result of the less-than-stellar reputation of insurance salespeople. For this reason, there is an entire section on the fourth secret—Insure Success—where you can learn how to eliminate the conflicts of interest in your insurance portfolio.

Mo' Money, Mo' Problems

The greater your success, the more complicated your situation. When your situation becomes more complicated, you will have a more difficult time keeping track of how changes in one area may influence the other parts of your planning. To illustrate how complexity grows exponentially when you add more components, consider the number of relationships that exist in groups of various sizes, shown in Table 9.

TABLE 9: How Many Personal Relationships Exist as Groups Grow

Members in Group	Unique Relationships	Relationships
2—Ann and Bob	1	Ann-Bob
3—Ann, Bob, Chris	3	Ann-Bob, Ann-Chris, Bob-Chris
4—Ann, Bob, Chris, Dave	6	Ann-Bob, Ann-Chris, Ann-Dave, Bob-Chris, Bob-Dave, Chris-Dave
5—Ann, Bob, Chris, Dave, Ed	10	Ann-Bob, Ann-Chris, Ann-Dave, Ann-Ed, Bob-Chris, Bob-Dave, Bob-Ed, Chris-Dave, Chris-Ed, Dave-Ed

The table above considers only direct relationships. You can appreciate that if something goes wrong with Ann's relationship with Bob, that there could be an indirect impact on Ann's or Bob's relationship with Chris or Dave. Suffice to say, business gets exponentially more complicated as you add people, business units, or areas of planning. You are going to need a great team of advisors to keep it all in line (or a healthy dose of morphine, so you just don't care if it isn't).

My Situation Isn't *That* Complicated

If you don't think that you have a complex set of goals already, consider the partial list of common financial planning concerns. How many of these are important to you?

1. Managing the growth of your assets
2. Managing lawsuit risks from employees, customers, and competitors
3. Protecting assets from eventual lawsuits
4. Managing investment risk while attempting to grow assets
5. Managing tax liabilities to maximize after-tax growth
6. Managing business succession and estate planning concerns;
7. Growing a business so you can sell it someday
8. Protecting family members against a premature death or disability
9. Protecting your family's inheritance against lawsuits, taxes, and divorce

If these are all on your to-do list for this afternoon, this week, or this month, you are going to need that morphine mentioned in the previous paragraph. I am not suggesting that you shouldn't want to address these concerns. I am merely saying that the only way to handle them all is by leveraging your team of advisors.

See Your Better Path

We have only 24 hours in a day. We are limited in the amount of resources we can access at any given time. Limited time and money create our unique capacity. Leverage is not about working harder. You will be much better served if you focus on working *smarter* without having to work *harder*. When we try too hard or stretch our resources too far, we can suffer catastrophic setbacks.

The key to safely expanding capacity is through leverage. Leverage allows you to get more done with less effort, in less time, and for less money. Think of leverage as the anti-child. Leverage gives you back everything that having children has zapped from you— energy, free time, and disposable income. When was the last time you had too much of any of those?

You can't turn back time with leverage, but you can use leverage to make your time more valuable. You can leverage education to increase your earning potential (or that of your family members or employees). You've learned the basic building blocks of leveraging employees and advisors to get things done for you. The advanced course will be offered in the fourth secret.

You can focus on finding ways to get more out of your assets, your people, and your resources. You can leverage your money, other people's money, and even your intellectual property. Once you save money, you can reinvest in ways either to make more money or to create additional leverage. This is the compounding effect of leverage that the most successful have mastered.

When you have all your levers in place, you will be primed to make serious progress on your ambitious goals. When you are moving that fast, you are bound to make some mistakes. The third secret is Expect, Prepare for, Then Welcome Failure. This section will teach you how to make sure that your educational experiences (others call them failures) will be only temporary setbacks on your road to outrageous success.

CHAPTER 5

The Third Secret: Expect, Prepare for, Then Welcome Failure

"Only those who dare to fail greatly can ever achieve greatly."

—ROBERT F. KENNEDY

You have ambitious goals. If you didn't, you wouldn't have chosen a book about leveraging success. You are dedicated. If you weren't, you would have put this book down after seeing the statistics. It is likely that fewer than one in 1,000 people will ever reach the level of success you have targeted for yourself. You accept the fact that reaching your goals will pose a major challenge—and you are willing to meet that challenge head-on. I love that!

You understand that you'll have to elevate your perspective so you can find a different path to success. When you reach your goals, people will say about you, "Nobody had *ever* done what he did, the way he did it. He was a true pioneer!" The thought of being seen as a visionary or pioneer is both exciting and motivating. It is one of the stronger drives I have, so I understand the allure very well. Before we talk about safe pioneering, let's look at the definition of the word "pioneer."

Pioneer (noun): a person who is among the first to explore or settle a new country or area. (verb): to develop or be the first to use or apply (a new method, area of knowledge, or activity)

Source: *Oxford Dictionaries*

Beginner's luck is no reliable blueprint for success. The quotes in this chapter teach the same valuable lesson. You will not succeed at everything. You will try many times before you succeed. The most successful people learn from their mistakes. The most successful people are more likely to credit their success to resiliency, grit, and determination than to intelligence, creativity, and personality.

I am hardly throwing stones from my glass house. You can call me Sy Sperling. Remember what he said in the Hair Club for Men television ads? He would show a picture of himself when he was bald and say, "I am not only the president, I am also a member." I started seven different companies in the past 20 years—I didn't sell one for millions of dollars until last year. I may be the only real estate investor to lose money in both the Los Angeles and Austin markets. It was my 13th book that was my first bestseller. I am even on my second marriage. Six years ago, I considered filing bankruptcy before borrowing hundreds of thousands of dollars from a friend to try to get everything straightened out. I am proud to say that it all worked out—but not without aggravation, frustration, and countless sleepless nights.

You are going to try to do something new. You are going to make mistakes. That may be very scary for many of you. You are likely reading this book because you have beaten the odds and are already in the top 1% of earners in America. Now you want to get to the next level, but you don't want to lose everything that you have worked so hard to accomplish. It probably feels like a game show, and I'm the host asking, "You can go home with $300,000 today *or* you can risk it all for a chance to win $1 million! What will you do?"

Nearly 15 years ago, I was taught a valuable lesson about taking risks, by an innovator in the financial services industry. J.K. McAndrews saw me speak at a national financial services conference. He hired me to come to Houston to teach his Mass Mutual agency some of the new retirement strategies I had developed for wealthy clients. I don't remember anything about that trip to Houston except the one profound question he asked, "What would you do if you knew you could not fail?"

J.K. and I had a lovely (and obviously memorable) conversation. We discussed the power of the question. He prodded me for my answers to his question. This isn't an easy question to answer at first, but the answers will tell you a lot about yourself.

> **"Success is stumbling from failure to failure with no loss of enthusiasm."**
>
> —WINSTON S. CHURCHILL

I generally pride myself on asking great questions, but J.K. had just asked me the best question I had ever heard. J.K. knew it was such a great question that he had it inscribed on a paperweight that is still on my desk. Whenever someone walks into my office and looks at it, an interesting conversation always ensues.

Now, this question is far from hypothetical. Don't think about this question in the same vein as, what would you do if you won the lottery? Winning the lottery is all about luck. Nothing you can do will increase the odds of one ticket's winning. To "not fail" at reaching your ambitious goals is an outcome that you control completely. You have not failed until you have stopped trying. So, to "not fail" means that every mistake will be only a minor and temporary setback, teaching you valuable lessons for the future. You just want to make sure that you put safeguards in place to avoid career-ending mistakes.

The most successful business owners and wealthiest families have made their share of mistakes. However, they all have one thing in common. They have all been able to avoid catastrophic financial losses. This is not a stroke of luck on their part, either. The most successful know that they will be taking chances. They know they will have multiple failures. They don't worry about failure—they expect it and plan for it.

By dedicating time and money to actively managing financial and legal risks, you will learn how to protect yourself, your company, and your family from the mistakes you are undoubtedly going to make. The end result is to significantly reduce the effect of downturns in *your personal economy*—allowing you to bounce back quickly and continue on your journey toward your ultimate success.

The third secret will explore financial disasters and litigation risks that threaten every business owner and wealthy family. These risks include personal and business risks as well as health and financial events. More specifically, they include:

1. Litigation against you, your company or your family
2. The premature death of someone in your family or in your business
3. A disability affecting someone in your family or your business

With the solutions in this section, you will learn how to protect first what you have already accumulated (i.e., your assets), and second, what you are building (e.g., your company or family office). In the third secret, I will show you how to protect your own ability to fuel greater success (i.e., your income or earning potential). In the sixth secret, we will focus on how to protect all of your life's work so you can be certain of the positive impact you have on your family, your community, and the world. You will learn how to leave a lasting legacy that will proudly bear your name.

As you read this section, pay attention to the asset protection secrets that have protected the most successful families and entrepreneurs for decades. With these safeguards in place, the question "What would you do if you knew you could not fail?" will no longer be rhetorical—it will be a prediction!

Do as I Say, Not as I Didn't Do

In 2002, I wrote a book titled *Wealth Protection: Build and Preserve Your Financial Fortress.* At that time, outrageous jury awards were leading to a medical malpractice crisis for physicians. Doctors were leaving medicine or moving to states with tort reform. At the same time, neurosurgeons and partners in law firms were quitting because they were making so much more money day trading. Everybody was worth a fortune on paper, and they wanted to protect their assets from crazy lawyers and anyone who would hire those lawyers on contingency. It was like the Wild West in many ways. Times sure have changed, but it still feels like the Wild West in other respects.

In *Wealth Protection*, I introduced the concept of *personal economy*. Everyone is concerned at some level with the world and national economies. The aggregate effect on business is referred to as *macro*economics. As you start looking at more specific groups (countries, then regions of countries, then states, then cities, etc.), you are said to be getting into *micro*economics.

People are most concerned about the ultimate microeconomy—their *personal economy*. Everyone feels bad when watching a *60 Minutes* pieces about people who lost their homes to bank foreclosures or about workers who lost their investments to a Ponzi scheme by Bernie Madoff or Allen Stanford. Those feelings pale in comparison to the feeling you would have if you lost *your* home or had *your* investment and retirement funds stolen by a criminal. In the introduction to that book, I talked about my mother's unfortunate circumstances.

Wealth Protection: My Earliest Experience

My stepfather, Tom Fogarty, died unexpectedly three years after he and my mother were married. You can't make this up—his life insurance paperwork was sitting on the dining room table waiting for a signature when he died. My mother ultimately lost her home and filed bankruptcy. This is a sad story, but I am proud to say that my mother, 30 years later (at the age of 70), had worked hard to save enough money to finally buy her own home again. She wanted to do it herself—and she did. Her resiliency and hard work are an inspiration to everyone around her, not just to her kids.

You would think that an author of asset protection books and someone with a front-row seat to financial devastation would have all his planning done way in advance, right? The cobbler's son appears to have no shoes. I had a personal experience that reshaped my appreciation that you can go from riches to rags very, very quickly.

Eight years ago, I went through a financially devastating divorce. The long, drawn-out process was even more devastating emotionally, since my daughter was younger than two years old at the time. To add insult to injury, my former business partners decided to go in a different direction and voted me out of the firm I had founded 15 years earlier. With little emotional strength for another legal battle, and no war chest to pay for an expensive fight in court, I came very close to filing bankruptcy. If it hadn't been for the generosity of former clients who had become close friends, I would have been out of the financial consulting field altogether with a blemish only the current president of the United States can wear with pride.

I had gone from making over $600,000 per year for multiple years in a row and living in a $1.5 million home in the hills overlooking Austin to making less than $50,000 and sleeping in a friend's guest room. It was humbling, to say the least. This is why I encourage you to take a look at the threat assessment section to figure out where the holes in your safety net are.

Threat Assessment—Litigation

You may choose to skim these questions to build an appreciation for how much this section might benefit you. For your convenience, there is also a link in the Additional Resources section at the end of this book to a form that you can print out and work on separately when you want to devote more time to this exercise.

- Do you own *any* valuable assets in your own name or jointly with a spouse?
- Do you own any personal, commercial, or investment real estate?
- Are you a physician, a lawyer, an architect, a real estate developer, or a contractor?
- Do you personally guarantee any personal or commercial loans or lines of credit?
- Do you own a business?
- Is your business a sole proprietorship, a partnership, or a limited liability company with only one owner?

- Does your business have any intellectual property, trademarks, copyrights, patents, valuable client information, or trade secrets?
- Do people in your community consider you to be rich or successful?
- Have you ever been, or do you think there is any chance of your being, sued by a partner, an employee, a vendor, or a customer?

If the answer to any of these questions is yes, then you should take asset protection seriously.

Protecting Your Assets

If you have traveled abroad, you have undoubtedly seen some impressive castles. Many of these ancient structures may have been called residences or places of worship, but it is rather obvious that the builder or owner was intent on keeping something inside safe from some people who were on the outside. While valuable possessions were safely inside the walls, their owners could enjoy them without threat of loss. This is exactly what we want to accomplish with asset protection planning.

No, I am not suggesting the next reality show, *Extreme Moat and Drawbridge*, in which wealthy families extend their extreme pools around the entirety of their homes and fill them with crocodilians, sharks, or other deterrents. Though watching that show would be much more interesting than sitting down with an asset protection attorney, you will be better served by utilizing legal and financial strategies to protect your assets—until the next economic collapse, at least.

The past few decades have given us one of the most significant periods of wealth accumulation in developed countries, especially in the United States and China. Asset protection is the structuring of one's assets in a way that discourages lawsuits and shields them from creditors. The goal of asset protection planning is simple, but achieving it can be easy and inexpensive or it can be quite difficult and extraordinarily costly. The most effective asset protection strategies integrate ideas from multiple disciplines and are reviewed regularly for adjustments and modifications.

In the appendices, you will find more detailed information about the most common asset protection tools. Here, I will share the hierarchy of asset protection tools and where they are best utilized. If you need additional assistance, feel free to contact me through JarvisTower.com. I will be happy to introduce you to someone in your state whom I have worked with in the past. This may help you streamline the process of protecting what you have so you can move on to achieving your goals.

Hierarchy of Protection

Though the amount of protection each state affords the assets of its residents may differ greatly, the general hierarchy of asset protection strategies is as follows:

State and Federal Exemptions

Federal and state laws exempt certain assets from creditors. This means that someone who has lost a judgment could file for bankruptcy, dismiss the creditor and all his claims, and *keep* those exempt assets.

- **Most retirement plans.** 401(k) plans, 153(b) plans, 457 plans, pensions, profit sharing plans, and IRAs are exempt from creditors. This means that you can file bankruptcy but nobody can touch your retirement plan assets. This is a nice benefit, but you can put only so much into a retirement plan. Further, these plans are built for rank-and-file employees, not for highly compensated people like you. For more advanced retirement strategies, make sure you read the fifth secret.

- **Primary residence (homestead).** In states like Texas and Florida, the protection is unlimited. You could own a $5 million home and still keep it after filing bankruptcy. Ironically, in states like California and New York, where homes can be very expensive, the homestead protection may be $150,000 or less of equity.

- **Life insurance and annuities.** You will learn about the power of the insurance lobby in the next secret. For your benefit, many states (Texas, New York, and Florida, just to name a few) offer unlimited protection of cash values inside insurance contracts. In Texas, I have a client who has insurance policies with over $10 million of cash value growing inside the policy free of any income tax and completely safe from creditors. Further, the family can borrow the cash value tax-free from the policy at any time. This concept has been referred to as "infinite banking" or "being your own bank."

  Infinite banking is very popular with clients who are concerned about lawsuit risk, who don't want to pay taxes on investments in the market, who want access to the money more easily than they would have if the money were in real estate or private equity, and who want to have some additional liquidity at the time of passing of certain family members. If you are unsure what protection your state affords insurance contracts, feel free to email JarvisTower and we will be happy to share that information with you.

- **Weird stuff.** Some states protect a car. Other states exempt an ox or a goat. Some will protect a blacksmith's hammer. These are fun but not particularly valuable to discuss in this short space.

Business and Personal Insurance

Having commercial insurance is useful, but it has its pitfalls. I have included an article about the pros and cons of property and casualty insurance in the Additional Resources. This will help you see some of the pitfalls that may result from relying solely on insurance. One quick tip is to talk to your homeowners insurance and auto insurance companies and ask them to look at both policies (even if they are with different insurance companies) and to quote you a $5 million or $10 million umbrella liability policy. This is a very inexpensive way to boost the protections from lawsuits arising from visitors to your home or from people hurt by your or (more likely) your kids' driving.

Family Limited Partnerships (FLPs) and Limited Liability Companies (LLCs)

These are the building blocks of asset protection. Though exemptions offer better protection and corporations and trusts have been around longer, FLPs and LLCs are much more powerful. They are the Swiss Army knives of planning. They can be used to own real estate, securities, operating businesses, intellectual property (copyrights, patents, and trademarks), and almost any other asset (except a primary residence or retirement plan).

For asset protection purposes, they have a very cool feature called "charging order protection." This means that if someone successfully sues you and gets a judgment against you, the owner of an LLC or an FLP, the creditor cannot force you to distribute assets from the LLC or FLP to satisfy the judgment. The creditor can only file a charging order against the entity, forcing it to redirect any future distributions to himself or herself. If you are the manager of the entity, would you ever schedule a distribution that you knew you wouldn't get? Right!

These structures allow you to separate ownership between voting and non-voting interests, so you can share the assets with children or other people whom you don't want to have the same amount of control that you want to preserve for yourself. You can also create preferred and common classes of interest. This is particularly valuable in the case of very advanced wealth transfer strategies—which will be described in the sixth secret.

Most business owners realize that they have four times the risk of employees. A very highly paid executive worries about protecting assets from personal financial and legal mistakes. A business owner has that same concern, plus three more:

If business owners don't properly employ asset protection strategies, they risk:

- Losing their business assets to business risks
- Losing their personal assets to business losses
- Losing business assets to personal lawsuits

Because of these added concerns, business owners often use one LLC to own safe personal assets (securities), another LLC to own each personal real estate property, and multiple LLCs for each operating business. The idea of segregating businesses is discussed later in this chapter. In the meantime, if you want to read more about some of the interesting benefits of LLCs and FLPs, see the Additional Resources section.

Trust the Trust, Not Your Kids

For asset protection planning, irrevocable trusts are key. We are not talking about a living trust. Living trusts are often referred to as A-B trusts, revocable trusts, or family trusts. These trusts can provide a little protection, but that protection happens only after someone dies—which is a price I don't think any of you should be willing to pay for a little protection.

Trusts are a separate entity. There is a grantor, who sets up the rules of the trust and funds it. The trustee is the person responsible for carrying out the wishes of the grantor. The beneficiaries are the ones who receive the assets, income, or use of assets in the trust. The trust can be structured in many ways, depending on the desired tax treatment. A few creative strategies will be covered in the sixth secret.

Assets in trust are not the same as personally held assets. This means that a lawsuit (including divorce) against the beneficiary, trustee, or even grantor of a trust cannot access the funds in trust. This can be a very valuable tool to help you protect your children without requiring them to sign prenuptial agreements and starting a fight with your beloved, if not starry-eyed, heirs.

In the past two decades, multi-generational (or "dynasty") trusts have become the rage. You can leave assets in a trust for multiple generations without subjecting your grandchildren to estate taxes when they inherit the remaining trust assets from your kids. This is a gift in the tax code that every wealthy family is utilizing. This is the ideal place for any assets you expect to appreciate considerably—the stock of a new business venture, family real estate heirlooms, or high-risk private equity. This way, all growth will happen outside your estate and not be subject to high estate tax liabilities that may not have been contemplated in your previous planning.

There is a really exciting trust that I have also taken advantage of in recent years. This is the trust that lets you, the entrepreneur, run your own business, control your own assets, and not worry about any estate tax liability when you leave those assets to your children. This is the beneficiary defective dynasty trust. You can learn more about this tool in the Additional Resources section.

To see which tools work best for protecting your assets and helping you reach your goals, you will want to work with your advisory team. It is important to assemble a team of advisors who have a wide range of skills and who are well aware of your comprehensive goals. Many tools can provide multiple benefits, saving you the costs and aggravation of duplication of efforts.

Protecting Your Business

Your business is the second most valuable asset you have, behind only your ability to work, build, and earn. Since you have already embraced the second secret, the importance of leverage, you know that you can never reach the highest levels of success by just working harder. You appreciate that a business is a great tool for leveraging employees, leveraging capital, and even leveraging ideas (when the team can turn them into reality). It's highly likely that the ambitious goals you created at the end of the first secret will involve some increased leverage of your current business, a future business you will start, or a strategic relationship with someone else's business.

Earlier, we discussed how business owners have four areas of concern for asset protection, whereas employees have only one. Businesses can create liabilities that threaten personal and business assets. Every person generates liability in day-to-day life. When a business owner drives a car, an accident could threaten personal and business assets. If you consider that many businesses have multiple owners, then the liability risk can grow exponentially.

When you consider that there is more to lose and many more ways to lose it when you are a business owner, you can see why it makes perfect sense for business owners to take steps to shield the business and all its assets as well. However, at JarvisTower we find that most business owners are so busy building the business that they ignore protecting the business assets. Another contributing factor is that most asset protection is done by estate planning attorneys. This planning is often done as a secondary benefit that accompanies wills and trusts, not as part of a global restructuring to maximize the value of a business at sale. Whether the blame falls on the business owner's failure to plan or the attorney's focus on personal assets, the fact is that most business assets are unnecessarily exposed. In an attempt to "stop being beige" and to see a better path, let's consider two strategies to protect your business and its assets.

Divide and Not Be Conquered: Asset Segregation

A dentist once told my kids, "You only really need to floss the teeth you want to keep." Similarly, asset protection is only really for the assets you don't want to lose in a lawsuit. Hopefully, we can all agree on the following assumptions before we move forward:

1. A litigious society necessitates the protection of assets.
2. Asset protection is not part of the traditional financial planning many firms offer.
3. Owning a business or investment real estate owners increases your risk.

There is an increased need to protect multiple assets or multiple properties from the various threats. This can be done through asset segregation using multiple legal entities.

There are three reasons to separate the ownership of the real estate and equipment (RE) from the operating business. First, the RE is an asset that should be isolated from any liability created by the business. Second, the RE itself may cause liability. That liability could be in the form of slip-and-fall claims by people coming and going on the premises or claims deriving from the equipment's injuring someone. If the RE and the business are operated by the same legal entity, all eggs are in the same basket. This means that the claim will be against an entity that has assets to lose.

By separating the RE from the business, you have asset-protected the business. By isolating the business from the real estate, you may have removed the premises liability and equipment liability created by the business's real estate. In doing so, each entity is protected from the other. This is the kind of planning that savvy affluent people undertake.

What Segregation Involves

Separating ownership simply involves creating a new LLC and transferring ownership of the real estate to it. Because the RE is no longer owned by the operating business, employees suing the business have no claim against this RE or the LLC that owns the RE. So long as the transfer to the LLC is done properly and the formalities of the new arrangement are respected, this protection will hold.

Your Financial Incentive

For simplicity's sake, we will assume that you have a single-owner business even though these techniques work equally well for businesses with multiple owners.

Let's say that you own your business RE through an LLC that is initially owned by you and your spouse. Your attorney will wisely guide you to create both voting and non-voting interests. Perhaps the voting interests represent 10% of the total interests, and the non-voting interests represent the other 90%. Over time, you and your spouse can gift non-voting ownership interests to your children. Your goal would be to remove 90% of the value from your estate, while maintaining 100% control of the LLC and the real estate inside it. This relatively simple strategy could save you tens of thousands of dollars of gift or estate taxes each year. Over a lifetime, that number could be significant to your family.

This asset-segregation strategy also helps you protect the assets of the business from lawsuits against any of your partners or employees. An additional benefit of this strategy is that it can be used to reduce your income taxes through income tax–sharing strategies. Once your children are of a certain age, some of this income will be taxed at their lower income tax rates.

Lastly, this strategy can also help you more efficiently structure the buyout of owners who retire. You could allow retired owners to retain ownership of the LLC that owns real estate or equipment or even intellectual property. This way, you could still pay Mom and Dad after they have left the business to you—reversing the strategy above and passing some income to your retired parents who are now in the lower tax bracket. This is much more efficient than having the high-earning family member pay the maximum amount of income tax and then support older and younger family members.

More advanced structures using multiple LLCs within a business can be utilized to protect assets and to enhance the enterprise value of the business—at the time of sale. This structure is outside the scope of this book but something we at JarvisTower encourage readers to contact us to discuss. For more advanced estate planning strategies, make sure you take the time to read the sixth secret. It will teach you how to leave a legacy that will extend far beyond your life expectancy.

Don't Gamble Away the Business: Bet Against Yourself!

Let me clarify a few things before we get too carried away. If you are an executive of a publicly traded company, please understand that I am not suggesting that you buy puts or sell calls on your company stock— then miss your earnings. Nobody wants to spend any time in the steel chateau for insider trading.

I am also not suggesting that you hedge your bets by investing in your competitors. I don't want you to do anything other than to attack your goals. My assistant Julia hung this quote in my office:

> **"The path to success is to take massive, determined action."**
>
> —TONY ROBBINS

You can run a seemingly perfect business. You can execute every element of your ambitious plan. You can hire and train great executives and managers. You can utilize every asset protection strategy you have read in this chapter. You can even implement all the strategies in the fifth secret to make sure your key people don't ever want to leave. You could become an entrepreneurial demi-god, gracing the covers of *Inc.*, *Entrepreneur*, and *Fast Company*.

While you should go after these ambitious goals, I am suggesting something other than *completely* reckless abandon. You already understand that you are taking significant risks to reach a higher level of success. Lawsuits and bad business decisions are not the only reasons businesses fail. What I am suggesting when I say, "Bet against yourself," is to take steps to ensure that your business will benefit from an absolute certainty—you will leave the business one day.

The Four Horsemen of the Entrepreneurial Apocalypse: Death, Disability, Disagreement, and Disinterest

According to *Business Insider*, there is an 80% chance that if you have a business partnership, it will break up. If you are the one in five that doesn't flame out, there is a 100% chance that each of you will eventually die. If you ignore the fact that you (and your partners) will someday leave your business, it will undoubtedly come back to bite you, your family, your partners, and your employees in the ass. Though it may appear to go against the idea of taking massive, determined action, it doesn't. We will spend more time in the sixth secret talking about your legacy, so right now we will just agree that it is not in anyone's best interest to see your company fall apart because of poor planning.

Have you and your partners ever asked yourselves the following questions?

- What will happen if and when any of my partners die? How will their families fare as owners of my company? Do I want them as new partners? How would I buy them out at that time? Do I have enough money to give them the price they think is fair?

- What will happen to my share of the business if I decide I want to exit the business or retire? Will my partners or employees have enough money to buy me out at a price I believe is fair?

- What will happen if any of my partners become disabled or get into messy divorces? Will I have to take on their spouses as partners?

- What will happen to my family if I die or become disabled? How can I be assured that they will get their fair share of the business value?

- Am I 100% sure that my family would be treated fairly by my surviving partners?

- Am I 100% sure that my partners' surviving family members would believe that my offers were fair and reasonable, or would they think I am trying to take advantage of them?

If you don't address the dissolution of any owner's interest in the company before the event occurs, partners and surviving family have no legally enforceable plan for how this transaction will take place. At a time when the family is grieving and possibly struggling to pay bills, members of that family will look to the surviving partners' business for help in their time of need. At the same time, the surviving partners may be struggling to get by without the services of a valuable owner. The last thing either of these two groups needs is a power struggle over money. In too many cases, the absence of the single most important business document, the buy-sell agreement, at the time of death or disability can cause bankruptcies of the families or millions in lost value when they are forced to sell the business—for pennies on the dollar.

The Ever-Important Buy-Sell Agreement

A buy-sell agreement is *the* agreement that all owners (of corporations, partnerships, LLCs, etc.) should sign to remove all the doubt arising from the aforementioned questions. The buy-sell agreement stipulates how the business will be valued at the time of one partner's death, disability, disagreement, or disinterest. The very small percentage of businesses that have successfully been transferred across generations universally are those in which the owners have had buy-sell agreements and transition plans drafted, signed, and funded. In addition, the agreements were regularly reviewed and amended as the businesses, ownership percentages, and family dynamics changed.

The document contemplates how the purchase of the departing partner's shares will be paid. There are various ways to structure buy-sell agreements, depending on the goals and circumstances of the owners and the business itself. In all arrangements, there are some basics regarding buy-sell agreements that can apply to any type of business.

Benefits to the Business and Remaining Owners

First, a properly planned buy-sell agreement will provide for the orderly continuation of the ownership and control of the business. This continuation should survive the death, disability, divorce, or bankruptcy of any owner and should provide for a seamless transition in the event any owner wants to retire and sell his or her ownership shares.

Second, the buy-sell agreement can prevent unwanted outsiders from becoming owners and can eliminate the need for negotiation with surviving spouses and children. The agreement may also perform the role of a succession plan by providing for the continuity or orderly succession of business management. Further, the buy-sell agreement is often used in conjunction with life insurance and disability insurance policies to effectively provide liquidity for the business to purchase the outstanding ownership interests of the disabled or deceased partner.

Perhaps most important, the buy-sell agreement guarantees that the remaining owners will continue to control the business and be able to participate in its future growth. This also prevents a competitor from purchasing ownership interests from a retired, disabled, or deceased owner or surviving family member who desperately needs the money. Thus, the buy-sell guarantees continuity of management in the business, ultimately making the business more attractive to customers, creditors, and employees.

Benefits to Each Owner

From the standpoint of a living business owner, the buy-sell agreement can provide the individual partner with the opportunity to negotiate and obtain the fairest or best price for his or her share of the business. In the case of retirement or disability, the agreement can be an additional source of funds for each owner.

Benefits to Family Members

The buy-sell agreement also benefits the family members in the case of death or disability in various ways. For a deceased owner's family, the existence of the buy-sell can assure the family or estate a liquid asset rather than an illiquid minority interest in a privately held business that would be difficult to sell. As mentioned earlier, this can be important because the surviving family may be burdened with estate tax payments. The agreement itself may provide a valuation of the business interest, which can be used for estate tax filing purposes. This may save the survivors the additional headache and expense of securing another valuation and fighting the Internal Revenue Service on that value.

If one owner becomes disabled, the buy-sell contract guarantees that the disabled owner's family does not have to become involved in the business to protect the family's interest. The buy-sell agreement can free the disabled owner and his family from the risk of future business losses, and create funds that may be used to pay medical bills and living costs.

This creates peace of mind, as the disabled owner will have retrieved any investment in the business and will not have to continue to worry about its future. Let's look at the quick case study of Tim and Al.

■ **CASE STUDY**

Tim and Al Are Tooling Along, Until They Aren't

Tim and Al are the owners of a building company with $100 million in annual revenue. Tim has the sales and marketing expertise, while Al runs the production side of the operation. Their overall profitability results from their joint efforts. If Tim were to die prematurely, Al would have to either hire a new employee or promote someone to fill Tim's position. A new hire would be unlikely to duplicate Tim's huge personality.

At the same time, Tim's widow would want to continue to take the same money out of the business that she and Tim received before Tim's death. In fact, if Tim's widow is raising a young family or has children in college, she may have to force a sale of the business at a distressed price just to meet her needs.

Maybe Tim's son is also in the business and has his own ideas about how things should be run. Perhaps Tim's wife wants to see Tim's son take over his father's place. It wouldn't matter that Junior is incompetent. This could create lots of problems for both families. Needless to say, it might be impossible for Al to continue to run a profitable business under such circumstances.

Unless you want to have to sell your business to pay your late partner's family or take on the spouse or child of your late partner as your new partner, you must plan. Only by planning can you and your partners answer these questions in a way that satisfies all parties, while enabling the business to be maintained. As mentioned earlier, the best tool for solving the dilemmas that arise from these questions is the buy-sell agreement in its various forms.

■ **CASE STUDY**

When Compassion Creates Chaos Among Professionals

While working with a profitable boutique West Coast law firm, I saw something new. Though it was new to me, and to the firm, I am guessing that it is relatively common. Most professional firms—of lawyers, doctors, architects, accountants—have similar rules. Because the practices are partnerships built on the billings of their partners, there is little room for partners to own a piece of the firm and to continue getting paid distributions after they stop working. Many partnership agreements call for partners to be "bought out" of their interests when they can no longer work. Specifically, this would include death, disability, and a mandatory retirement age.

One of this West Coast firm's beloved senior partners, Sheila, had a terminal form of cancer. As a result, she could not meet her billing requirement. Per the agreement, she should have been bought out of her interests. Unfortunately, as is the case with many professional firms, the partner equity is a very small amount. Sheila had $350,000 of equity in her capital account. However, her anticipated annual bonus that year was expected to be north of $10 million.

The firm decided not to vote Sheila out of her shares and to wait until after the next large distributions and bonuses were made. This was absolutely the right thing to do on a human level and a business level. When Sheila passed away, the surviving family maintained a good relationship with many of the partners in the firm. The relationship is still strong to this day. But this situation uncovered a problem.

A benefits consultant and an employment attorney pointed out that the decision to not enforce the partnership agreement for Sheila could be seen as a precedent-setting act, protecting departing partners' future distributions. Though the senior partners never wavered in their position with Sheila, they did acknowledge that Sheila's lack of adequate disability insurance did factor into their decision to not stop paying her when she was sick.

What we came up with as a solution has since benefitted many medical and law practices. I engaged Dan Aceti of Executive Benefits Group in Charlotte, North Carolina, to engineer an innovative disability program with Lloyd's of London. He was able to secure up to $300,000 per month of benefits for the partners of this highly profitable practice. He was also able to get them guaranteed issue coverage (no physicals or lab tests needed). The firm then required that every partner carry at least $60,000 per month of disability income insurance.

The logic behind this idea was solid. The application was very creative. The firm would enforce its partnership termination clause in the future—when partners could no longer work. Since departing disabled partners would now earn no less than $720,000 per year (tax free) for at least five years, the firm wouldn't feel guilty letting them go. They said that any partner should be able to handle the financial rigors of transitioning out of practice with at least $3.6 million of tax-free benefits over a five-year period.

The Need for a Coordinated Team

Creating a buy-sell arrangement that fits a specific business requires expertise and experience. Expertise in areas of corporate and business law, tax law, innovative and customized insurance products, and the valuation of businesses is an *absolute* requirement. Just as important is experience in dealing with different owners and the ability to negotiate and draft an agreement that meets the needs of all parties involved. Too often business owners make one of two mistakes in deciding who should oversee the creation of a buy-sell arrangement:

- Some chose a friend who is a lawyer to create the strategy and draft the document rather than an expert in the area.

- Some do not have a coordinated team to implement the plan.

A coordinated buy-sell team would involve the following:

1. An attorney who has experience creating these types of arrangements
2. A life insurance professional who has access to specialty products (if there are any health concerns to navigate)
3. A disability insurance expert who has worked with Lloyd's of London
4. A business appraisal firm whose expertise may be needed on an ongoing basis for annual business valuations

Once you protect your business assets for your own use, and you protect your business so that it can continue to create leverage for all of the owners and their families, you will be well protected.

See a Better Path

When my son, Tyler, entered high school, my dad said, "He is going to make mistakes…lots of them. It's your job to make sure none of them are game-ending mistakes." Life is an interactive learning process. You must try to succeed, allow yourself to fail, then pick yourself up and try again. Thomas Edison once said, "I have not failed. I've just found 10,000 ways that won't work." Hopefully, a light bulb went on in your head as you read that one.

It should be easy to understand why so few people are successful. Even if you beat the odds and achieve a high level of success, you may spend most of your time trying to innovate to fight back competitors— just to maintain your level of success. All that time, you will be exposed to personal and commercial threats to your family wealth and business assets. These risks include personal and professional lawsuits, premature death, and disability.

By looking at the structure of your personal and business assets as an important ingredient in your recipe for success, you will avoid career-ending mistakes. Segregating assets, maximizing exempt assets, and reviewing the overall structure annually with a multi-disciplinary team of advisors are all important takeaways. Layering a properly crafted and fully funded buy-sell agreement will be the most effective asset protection strategy you use. I say this because every other mistake can be fixed after the fact—and every partner leaves his business only once. Any mistakes that occur then can't be fixed after the fact.

Now that you have protected yourself, we can move forward knowing that any setback you suffer today will not be a failure. Let's move ahead to the fourth secret: Insure Success. In that chapter, you will not only learn how to choose the best products for your asset protection plans, but you will also learn how to use the underwriting profits and sales commissions from the insurance industry to fuel some of your income initiatives.

CHAPTER 6

The Fourth Secret: Insure Success

"There are worse things in life than death. Have you ever spent an evening with an insurance salesman?"

—WOODY ALLEN

Have you recently received a large check from an insurance company to rebuild a burned-down home, to replace a car wrecked by a teenaged driver, or to provide income replacement to a family after the passing of a loved one? If the answer to all three questions is no, then you undoubtedly find insurance to be boring.

I completely understand what you are thinking. I have spent the better part of the past 25 years trying to get out of the insurance industry. It's not sexy. It's actually the opposite of interesting. You don't believe me? Consider this scenario. Someone sits next to you on the plane and asks, "What do you do?" If I want to be social and have a conversation, I generally say, "I write books," or "I solve problems," or "I'm the 'Giraffe CFO.'" Any of those three answers generally leads to a longer conversation. If I have a lot of work to do or I am delusional enough to think I might actually sleep on the plane, I respond with, "I sell insurance." That last line gets me all the peace and quiet I could ever want.

Even billion-dollar investors in the insurance industry find insurance to be painstakingly boring and the subject of much ridicule.

In September of 2017, I was introduced to a partner in a $19 billion private equity firm that focuses on insurance. He greeted me at the meeting by asking, "How did you end up in the ghetto of financial services?"

Believe it or not, I was not meeting with the only insurance-focused private equity firm. Apollo Global Management, the Private Equity Group of Ares, Blackstone Group, Stone Point Capital, and The Carlyle Group made a splash by investing billions of dollars in financial services and insurance-based acquisitions. Other diversified financial services operations, like BlackRock and Guggenheim Partners, have spent billions of dollars to purchase insurance companies. If none of these names impresses you, then you need only one name: Warren Buffet.

Why Does Warren Buffett Like Insurance Companies?

These companies are attractive because of their float, or cash with a near-zero cost of capital, which comes from the insurance premiums insurance companies collect every month. It is a good source of other people's money that Warren Buffett can use to make acquisitions and other types of investments interest-free.

There are also tax benefits to doing so, for corporate income tax rates are typically lower than personal income tax rates. Thus, using insurance companies as investment vehicles lowers the tax that Buffett has to pay on capital gains.

Insurance is boring and unsexy, but it can be very profitable. Don't take my word for it. There are billions of dollars of private equity flooding the insurance industry. One of the wealthiest men in the world has 18% of his $75 billion net worth tied up in one insurance company (Berkshire Hathaway). Warren Buffett's boring insurance company stock appreciated by 20.8% per year from 1965 to 2016. If you can get past the boring parts and you aren't too sexy for solid profitability and reliable cash flows, you too can learn how to insure your own success as well.

What the Hell Do I Know About Insurance?

I am no Warren Buffett, but I do have something valuable to add. In my 20s, I worked as an actuary, calculating and filing rates for large insurance companies. This gave me the opportunity to work with many insurance regulators in various state insurance departments. That experience landed me the job of creating two Vermont-domiciled insurance companies for one of the world's largest automobile manufacturers.

After trying to escape the insurance industry via business school (at UCLA), I was sucked back into insurance to assist business owners who wanted to build and manage their own insurance companies. I handled various domestic and international corporate formations, their complicated annual filings, and complex reinsurance arrangements before finally getting out by selling my insurance management business in 2016.

To make matters worse, I couldn't even "moonlight" in an interesting way. A friend of mine, Art Markman, is much better at this than I am. By day, he is the professor of human dimensions of organizations at the University of Texas. By night, he is a jazz musician wailing on his saxophone. That sounds fun! When I wasn't helping business owners integrate insurance company businesses into their umbrella of companies, I was handling their exciting ... wait for it ... life insurance challenges.

Most entrepreneurs and family offices don't trust their insurance agents, so they would ask me if I could help them understand the insurance proposals. Inevitably, I would find some oversight or inefficient structure in the original design. My alternative approach would either save them quite a bit of money or allow their corporations to turn these expenses into assets. In either case, they were very grateful. As a result, I built a million-dollar part-time life insurance business. Not as exciting as playing for a blues band, but a bit more profitable.

What this means for you is that I have experience with property and casualty, life, and health insurance. I also have spent time working at my home office, interacting with regulators, and sitting down with customers. I have worked with families and with CFOs to find better solutions. I have represented both the buyer and the seller on a multitude of insurance transactions. I know how the companies make money, what the regulators look to prevent, and what the clients hope to achieve with insurance products. I may in fact have the single most boring expertise in the world, but that experience is going to pay dividends for you. Right here. Right now. You can get the benefit of 25 years of pain with just 25 minutes of reading.

When you're done, you may actually want to read it again!

If You Can't Beat 'Em, Join 'Em

According to the Insurance Information Institute (III), the insurance industry in the United States is the largest in the world. Net written premiums in 2015 exceeded $1.2 trillion, with life and health insurers accounting for 55% and property and casualty (P&C) insurers accounting for 45%. As of 2015, there were 5,926 insurance companies in the United States, according to the National Association of Insurance Commissioners (NAIC).

Insurance is a huge part of the financial services sector, contributing close to 40% of the total gross domestic product (GDP) of the financial institutions. Insurance carriers and related activities contributed $450.3 billion, or 2.6%, of the US GDP in 2014, and insurance companies employed 2.6 million people that year, according to the Bureau of Economic Analysis.

Not impressed? Have you ever seen the MetLife Tower or New York Life building in New York City? How about the Prudential building or the Hancock Tower in Boston? Chicago's tallest building is the Willis Tower. Three more of the tallest are the Aon Center, John Hancock Center and Two Prudential Plaza. The Cleveland Indians play at Progressive Field. The Seattle Mariners call Safeco Field home, while the Rangers play at Globe Life Park. The New York Jets and New York Giants play at MetLife Stadium. This is a partial list to show you that insurance companies play a big role in real estate and sports—both very lucrative and expensive arenas.

Have you ever heard of the golden rule? "Those with the gold make the rules." If that is the case, then insurance might as well be the fourth branch of the government. According to the company S&P Global Market Intelligence, total cash and invested assets of all insurance companies totaled $5.2 trillion in 2015.

If you don't believe the golden rule, consider the following statistics. From 2009 through 2016, the insurance industry spent between $150 million and $170 million annually on lobbying efforts. In the past ten years, $1.5 trillion has been spent on insurance lobbying! Might this be a reason why the insurance companies get favorable tax treatment and are such attractive investment vehicles?

It doesn't matter why the insurance industry is so large. It is. If you are running a business or managing a family office, you have two choices when it comes to insurance. First, you can continue delegating this boring commodity purchase to someone else in your organization. Second, you can take a second to contemplate why one of the richest men in the world loves insurance companies and why insurance companies control so much of the wealth in this country. If you are willing to look at insurance differently, you might see a better path to success that includes leveraging some of the benefits insurance has to offer you.

The Whole Enchilada—Own It Outright

Warren Buffett may be the most famous, but he certainly is not the only wealthy investor to see the benefits of owning an insurance company. This became clear to me 25 years ago. When I was working at Liberty Mutual, our firm's biggest client was UPS. We handled its captive insurance company that insured workers' compensation risk for employees. When UPS said jump, the entire building at 175 Berkeley Street came off its foundation. After working there for a few years, I received a call from an actuarial recruiter who had been trying to pry me away from my great job. He asked me, "How would you like to launch an insurance company for one of the largest companies in the world?" With the hopes of being the youngest insurance CEO in the country, I took the job. Less than a year later, I had helped the world's largest auto manufacturer's Japanese world headquarters, California office and Michigan-based partner collaborate on two new Vermont-domiciled insurance companies.

As a 26-year-old with a 100-second attention span, I left the Japanese company with its 100-year business plan for the greener pastures of business school at nearby UCLA. After graduating, I was lured back to the insurance ghetto. There was a malpractice crisis in healthcare. Insurance was so expensive that doctors were actually leaving practices in Nevada for California and its lower cost of living (yes, you read that correctly) or practicing "bare" (without any insurance). I had written a book on asset protection for physicians with an attorney partner and was now working on finding affordable insurance for physicians. Risk retention groups (RRGs) were popular ways to create doctor-owned insurance companies to manage and shift risk.

When tort reform eliminated the high prices of medical malpractice coverage, the captive insurance industry didn't miss a beat. Businesses were looking for ways to manage unusual risks that were not being handled efficiently by traditional insurance channels. Companies were experiencing explosive growth in the late 1990s and again in the mid- to late 2000s. The new worldwide economy led to international expansion—which created all-new risks for many businesses. The World Wide Web led to e-commerce and even greater threats—which the slow-moving insurance industry was not equipped to handle.

In the absence of adequate commercial insurance, companies started looking for risk management solutions in the form of self-owned, or captive, insurance companies. This gave them the benefit of protecting or shielding operating assets from insurance company assets. For the savvy, this also created a tax-efficient, low-cost (of capital—see Warren Buffett's quote above) method of improving cash flow. With a fast-growing economy, these captives allowed businesses to stockpile a war chest for future losses and reinvest those funds into very lucrative investments. Of course, everything was a lucrative investment back then...until it wasn't.

Before I sold my insurance management business and got out of this business in 2016, I had the fortunate experience of working with six captive managers. In my two decades in that space, I worked with hundreds of business owners on various insurance brokerage, insurance management, and reinsurance solutions. What follows are some of the best practices I witnessed.

What Does Owning an Insurance Company Mean?

First, the ideal role of an insurance company that you own is to supplement existing insurance policies. This can include risks that your insurance carrier will not underwrite—because you have had a bad experience or because you don't want to pay the increased cost of a more comprehensive policy. Your company can also cover losses above a certain amount or can cover the deductibles or co-insurance payments that many commercial policies require the insured to pay.

Excess protection gives you additional peace of mind. The company and its owners would not be wiped out by a lawsuit award that exceeds traditional coverage limits. Because successful businesspeople who own businesses are concerned about all types of lawsuits—from product liability to environmental claims to employee lawsuits—this protection can be significant. Running a business is not for the faint of heart, as new risks seem to pop up every year. In recent years, there has been enormous growth in the captive insurance space for both cyber coverage and health insurance. The 2017 Equifax cyber breach is just one of many high-profile cases that could have sent a smaller company out of business. With Obamacare, the skyrocketing costs of health insurance have been very difficult for many businesses. We will examine one case study shortly.

Owning your own insurance company gives you the flexibility of using customized policies that may not be available from large third-party insurers. As an example, we can look back to the medical malpractice crisis. In some states, the amount of insurance coverage is something that lawyers can

> **"Insurance is the only product that both the seller and buyer hope is never actually used."**
>
> —UNKNOWN

submit as evidence to a jury. Since many clients fear that a jury will award the insurance coverage amount easily, clients and brokers found an interesting solution. They crafted a liability policy that would pay the client's legal fees and allow full choice of attorney for defense, but would not be available to pay creditors or claimants (what we call *shallow pocket* policies). This prevents the client from appearing to be a *deep pocket* (a prime lawsuit target). Avoiding this appearance can be a valuable asset protection strategy today.

Owning your own company offers you the flexibility to add coverage for liabilities excluded by traditional general liability policies, such as wrongful termination, harassment, or even Americans with Disabilities Act violations. Given that the awards in these areas can be greater than $1 million per case, savvy businesspeople understand the value of having their own insurance company for this benefit alone. Let's look at two case studies.

■ **CASE STUDY**

Chantal's International Affair

Chantal owns an international technology consulting firm with offices in the United States and Canada. She has 100 employees in each country. Chantal feels she is paying too much for her group's health insurance. She is a strong and compassionate leader and doesn't want her people to shoulder the outrageous burden of rising health insurance costs in the United States. As a Canadian citizen, she firmly believes everyone deserves fantastic health insurance. But she doesn't want to give away all the firm's profit to insure her employees. She was looking for a better path.

A highly respected insurance agency in Dallas put together a great program for Chantal. International tax experts at one of the nation's 20 largest law firms were able to help her navigate some international insurance tax and insurance laws. The result was a custom-crafted third-party commercial insurance plan with her own insurance company as a partner to the program. By increasing deductibles to the commercial carrier, Chantal was able to reduce her costs. She paid the savings to her own insurance company, for surplus policies that covered the gaps that the commercial insurance left.

Chantal was very excited that her excess coverage through her own insurance company allowed her to expand her coverage to include seeing her favorite doctor—who was not part of the commercial insurer's network. This creative combination of commercial and captive insurance solutions risk allowed Chantal to lower her total insurance costs, improve the overall health insurance coverage for her US-based employees, and preserve the personal relationship she had developed with her own doctor over the years.

■ **CASE STUDY**

Endorsing Insurance as a Solution

Justin is a professional golfer, making more than $10 million per year in salary and endorsements. As with any athlete, the risk of an injury's interrupting or ending his career is significant. Justin would like to insure against this risk. While many of his fellow tour players are advised to simply get an insurance policy from a specialty lines carrier such as Lloyd's of London, Justin got better advice.

Justin and his largest endorser, an apparel company, are most concerned with a career-ending injury, not a less serious one. They worked together on a very creative solution that involves an insurance company created by both Justin and the apparel company. The apparel company lent the insurance company $10 million to afford the company the assets it needs to provide ample coverage to Justin. The company then wrote policies to Justin, covering his loss of income from all types of injuries (knees, ankles, wrists, hands, back, and so forth). A reasonable premium for Justin is about $1 million per year, given his age and pre-existing conditions.

Because of the low-interest-rate environment, the term of the loan from the apparel company is 3%, and the term of the loan is for Justin's lifetime. Because Justin is so young, the collateral life insurance policy for the loan costs him less than $100,000 per year. If Justin stays healthy, most of the $10 million capitalization will find its way to him—along with his $1 million premium payments and their invested gains.

The insurance company also issued a $10 million "loss of key person" policy to the apparel company. If the company loses Justin as a key endorser of its products, the insurance company must pay it for the loss. This solidified the relationship between Justin and the apparel company. The positive impact on the financial statements of the apparel company is outside the realm of this book. However, it is safe to say that the relationship between the two parties was improved on both sides with this very creative use of insurance in place of a traditional endorsement deal.

When a client fully understands the benefits of insurance company ownership, the question often shifts from, "Why am I bothering with this boring shit?" to something that more closely resembles, "If I am going to use insurance to protect against risk, why give away the potential profitability, asset protection, and equity-building benefits when I don't have to?"

Let's examine a few of the benefits of having a captive insurance company (CIC) more closely.

- *Safer than a rainy day fund.* Because our society has become so litigious, many non-savvy affluent clients have been self-insuring against potential losses such as the ones named above. These clients have simply saved funds, which will be used to pay any expenses that arise if a risk becomes a reality. This is the proverbial *rainy day fund.* While a rainy day fund may prove wise, the client would be better off using a CIC to insure against any such risks. Premiums paid to the CIC are statutorily protected from the creditors of the operating company. This is a much safer alternative.

- *No loss of control.* When hundreds of thousands or millions of dollars are involved, every business owner undoubtedly wants to maintain control of the money. Owners typically maintain all control of their insurance companies' assets.

- *Avoids land mines.* Some insurance company structures may offer significant tax benefits. Companies properly structured under Internal Revenue Code Section 831(b) may not be required to pay income taxes on underwriting profit. Though this benefit does help properly structured companies stockpile tax-efficient reserves for future claims, the IRS has been very concerned with business owners who do not follow the guidelines properly. A recent tax court case, *Commissioner v. Avrahami*, illustrates some of the concerns. Intrigued businesses should consult with a team of advisors who have experience with these arrangements.

How Can You Set Up an Insurance Company?

Creating your own insurance company requires expertise in insurance, law, tax, and regulatory compliance. Many large and specialty law firms have insurance experts who can help you navigate these waters. State insurance departments grant insurance manager licenses to firms that specialize in this type of work. The two largest domiciles for captive insurance are Vermont and Bermuda. Others domestic domiciles of significant size include Delaware, Utah, and South Carolina, among others. *Captive Review* magazine is an industry publication that can also give you valuable information and lists of professionals who work in this space.

Take a Small Piece—Be the Middle Man

So, you don't want to be the next Warren Buffett and own an insurance company. I completely understand. The profit margin on most insurance companies runs around 5% to 8% per year. If you consider that there is a way to get a big piece of that profit without having to come up with all the capital needed for buying or starting an insurance company, you may want to try that option on for size.

We saw in the previous section that insurance companies are some of the largest companies in the world. Prudential, MetLife, and John Hancock are household names. Insurance is so big that even the middlemen are huge companies. Consider the following property and casualty brokerage firms:

TABLE 10: Top Insurance Brokers (by Annual Revenue)

Company	2015	2013
Marsh & McLennan Companies	$6.33 billion	$5.1 billion
Aon	$6.05 billion	$6.1 billion
Willis Towers Watson	$3.98 billion	$2.05 billion
Arthur J. Gallagher & Co.	$2.71 billion	$1.2 billion
BB&T	$1.68 billion	$932 million
Brown & Brown	$1.66 billion	$382 million
Wells Fargo Insurance Services	$1.32 billion	$960 million
HUB International	$1.15 billion	$932 million
USI Insurance Services	$1.03 billion	$390 million
Lockton Companies	$996 million	$791 million

You may have heard of a number of these companies. Look at the size of them. These are merely the middlemen, albeit international powerhouse middlemen.

TABLE 11: Largest Independent P&C Brokers by 2016 Revenue

HUB International	$1.1 billion
Lockton Companies	$1 billion
Alliant Insurance Services	$656 million
USI Insurance Services	$575 million
AssuredPartners	$547 million
Confie Seguros	$515 million
Acrisure	$479 million
BroadStreet Partners	$339 million
NFP Partners	$214 million
Integro Group Holdings	$189 million

Source: *Insurance Journal*

You probably recognized all the names of the insurance companies in Table 10. You probably don't recognize more than one or two of the ten in Table 11. What does that say about insurance brokerage? In 2013, the top 150 brokerage groups (for non-life business) earned global revenues of $28.5 billion. Aon topped the list in 2013 with $6.1 billion earned. Being the middleman is big, big business.

If you consider that 10% of property and casualty premiums are commissions, and that most insurance companies' profits represent a percentage of that commission, there has to be a significant premium placed on the securing of the business—selling!

To help you understand the value the industry puts on selling, I want to first put something into perspective for you. There is an entire industry commission split grid that contemplates the collaborative efforts of the multiple salespeople. The splits are basically:

TABLE 12: Million-Dollar Round Table (MDRT) Commission Split Grid

Client introduction	20%
Data gathering	20%
Proposal drafting	20%
Closing (selling)	20%
Servicing	20%

If I were to meet you and gather some data from you, then send it to another broker, I would be entitled to 40% of the commissions from your insurance sale. I'm not arguing about the fact that someone will pay me to send business. But I wonder what that might look like from the business owner's standpoint. If you are a business owner and you want insurance, then you certainly *could* introduce yourself. You have all the data and can give it to your broker. Shouldn't those functions allow you to keep 40% of the commission?

Wait! The insurance industry has put in a stopgap to protect itself. There are rules against "rebating" that all agents must adhere to in most states. You may not induce people to do business with you by paying them. I guess I understand that people can't "buy business," but isn't that what every other industry does? These are commodity products that have department-of-insurance-approved commissions. The rules essentially say that you can't do anything special to differentiate yourself—and you especially can't reduce your fees for the services you provide. Odd.

I love to push the envelope, but I don't want to do anything illegal. I looked for a better way to differentiate myself with my clients. This was part of the solution that I was alluding to in my bestselling book, *Mastering the Art of Success* (which I wrote with Jack Canfield and others). As part of a business consulting fee, I encouraged my clients to get properly licensed as insurance agencies. In many cases, I helped them do this. Then we set up fully disclosed commission split agreements between my agency and theirs. We then found a way to turn the expense of an insurance policy—health, workers' compensation, commercial liability, auto, life, disability, long-term care, etc.—into an income item for the clients.

If you are a holding company, an investment company, or a private equity firm, and you control a number of businesses, this agency-owning model can generate hundreds of thousands of dollars of additional annual income. Further, because the client owns the agency, the fear of the unknown ("How much is the insurance company making? Am I being screwed? What other things could I buy?" etc.) goes away. This has been a wonderful model for many of my company's clients. Yes, I stand to make less income per sale than my colleagues in the insurance industry. But isn't it the job of anyone in the service industry to try to find ways to better serve the clients?

Whether you like the idea of owning your own insurance company or you don't, the idea of owning part of the agency or brokerage should be on your radar. This will help you eliminate the fear of the unknown, since you will now be on the other side of the table due to the nature of your licensing. With more information, you will always be better prepared to make better decisions. This is a classic example of elevating your perspective to see a better path. If JarvisTower can be of any assistance in helping you take a piece of the $28 billion brokerage pie and putting it on your plate, please don't hesitate to contact us.

What Aren't You Seeing?

Magicians would tell you that the key to all magic is mastering the art of deception. This is true for any pocket trick or large stage production. *Misdirection* is a form of deception in which the attention of an audience is focused on one thing in order to distract its attention from another. Managing the audience's attention is the aim of all theater; it is the foremost requirement of theatrical magic. The term is used to describe either the effect (the victim's focus on an unimportant object) or the sleight of hand or patter (the magician's speech) that creates it.

That's interesting and ironic at the same time. Misdirection is the main reason why most businesses and families have such inefficient insurance and benefits plans. Insurance is a commodity product. Insurance is a necessary cost of doing business. You, Mr. or Ms. CEO, should go about your business—there is nothing to see here. This insurance and benefits stuff is something to defer out to someone in human resources, to an administrative person, or to someone in the family whose qualification is being reasonably organized and capable of filling out paperwork. This misdirection has kept top executives' attention away from these potential areas of differentiation.

As I write this in September 2017, I can tell you from firsthand experience that the majority of the insurance brokerage firms mentioned earlier in this chapter are on an acquisition spree. You may find insurance boring, but private equity firms are spending billions on insurance-based acquisitions. The term they use to describe business that stays on the books for a long time is "sticky business." They love the recurring revenue of health insurance and employee benefits because they are very sticky. As a result, the multiples they are paying for this very sticky business are very, very high relative to in past years. We know that insurance is not interesting. We know that the products are very heavily regulated. We know that nearly every business has to buy these products. These should be very low-priced, low-margin commodities. But somehow, the insurance companies and the brokers seem to be making a lot of money brokering commodity products— and overpaying like crazy to buy companies that are in this space. All of this just isn't consistent with the basics of economic theory.

Abracadabra! Turn Expenses into Assets

Hopefully, you have read enough to pique your interest. Insurance may be boring, but if you take some time to understand how some products can be utilized, you may be able to make your CFO, controller, and bankers very, very happy. Imagine if you could slightly alter the products you are already purchasing with these results:

1. A reduction in expenses, increasing EBITDA on the income statement
2. An increase in assets, improving shareholder equity on the balance sheet

Doing this will improve the ratios your bankers will be looking at for your covenants. It may improve a valuation or rating you receive from an outside entity. It will undoubtedly increase the amount of money a potential buyer will pay you. Every buyer understands that, all other things being equal, the same company is worth more when it reduces expenses, increases net income, and increases its assets on its balance sheet.

So, how do we turn expenses into assets? There are a number of ways that we have pioneered at JarvisTower. A detailed analysis of how we turn compensation and bonuses into assets will be included in the fifth secret. Make sure you keep reading after you finish this section. Now, we are going to focus on a simple way to make your financials look better by making a slight alteration to your insurance planning. Consider the one contract every business must have—the buy-sell agreement.

If you have multiple partners, you need a buy-sell agreement with the properly funded life and disability insurance on all partners. If your business has only one owner, then you likely need substantial key man life insurance and key man disability insurance to satisfy investors, lenders, or vendors. Without the proper agreements and adequate insurance, a death, disability, or disagreement could put the company out of business. Most businesses consider the cost of these insurances to be an operating expense—an unavoidable cost of doing business. That does not have to be the case.

■ CASE STUDY

William

William is a successful 50-year-old entrepreneur. He had been asked by a group of investors to run their new venture, converting a coal-fired power plant into a green-energy facility. The deal had been financed with a combination of debt and equity. The lenders wanted to make sure that there was key man insurance of $20 million on William. The initial premium estimates for 20-year-term insurance were $60,000 per year. This $60,000 annual expense would have been a deductible operating expense, but an expense nonetheless. If the lenders paid 20 years of premiums, the total outlay would have been $1.2 million.

They were considering pulling the trigger on this particular strategy, but called us to see if we had any alternative strategies to consider. We looked at a rather creative universal life policy. This is permanent insurance, not term insurance. The premium for this policy was much higher, $190,000 per year. The total outlay for this policy over 20 years would be $3.8 million. William quickly asked, "What I am missing?" The higher-priced policy has a "return of premium" rider in year 20. In the 20th year, the owner can choose to continue the policy or cancel it and receive 100% of the premiums back. Though the company will initially be out $2.6 million more with the new policy, it will get it all back at the end of the term. The company will save $1.2 million in total expenses over the 20 years.

William then asked, "What is the difference to the investors when the company sells?" That's another great question. The second policy is not an expense; it is an investment. The company's EBITDA (earnings) will actually be $60,000 higher each year. If the company hopes to sell for a multiple of 12 times earnings, the second insurance policy will help generate a sale price that will be $720,000 higher. In addition, the insurance asset will be worth up to $1.2 million more than the pure expense term policy. William then said, "So, buying the more expensive policy actually ends up being worth $2 million more to all of us who own the company."

Though $2 million is significant value to create for a business, it could have been much more. William was rather young, and we were working with insurance on only one executive. If there were three or four partners who were in their 60s or 70s, the benefit to the company might have been $20 million or more at sale. If you consider non-qualified deferred compensation or unfunded defined-benefit plans at law firms or accounting firms, you can have dozens or hundreds of participants. In those cases, of which we are currently working on a few, the benefit to the company or partnership could be in excess of $100 million just by changing the structure of the arrangement and utilizing specially designed products. This will be discussed in greater detail in the next section.

See a Better Path

Most businesses focus primarily on making money. The top-line revenue is the driver of the business. Analysts and investors talk about increases in units sold, gross revenues, or market share as badges of honor. Once the business achieves a certain threshold, meteoric growth is no longer sustainable. When there is little growth left to achieve, businesses are considered to be mature. The executives begin to look at cutting expenses as a way to continue to improve profit margins (and increase the value of their stock and stock options).

Insurance (other than health insurance) is usually very low on the list of items to review for potential cost savings. Life insurance hits the radar less than a stealth bomber does. Only five of the nearly 5,000 business owners I have spoken with have even thought about adding insurance revenue to their businesses. Nobody seems to think that insurance is an opportunity, yet one of the wealthiest men in the world (Warren Buffett) has built a $75 billion fortune through insurance. Insurance-focused private equity firms with funds totaling hundreds of millions of dollars are out there making investments. Billions of dollars are being spent to acquire insurance assets. If these rich and successful investors are looking at insurance as an opportunity, perhaps you may benefit from putting it on your radar.

Don't bother talking to the large brokerage companies or the home office representatives to find creative solutions. They have more employees in more locations suffering through more infrastructure and inefficiency than you or I will ever have. Looking for innovation from the same people who haven't given you any creative insurance ideas over the past 20 years is just plain silly. If they had anything interesting, they would have showed you already. If they knew how to save you (or make you) money and didn't share those ideas with you, wouldn't that be criminal? They may not have a fiduciary relationship with you, but aren't you looking for advisors who will put their interests at least on par with yours in your professional relationships?

When you are ready to see how insurance can work for you, instead of you working for your insurance companies and insurance brokers, you can consider a few options:

- Owning your own insurance company to keep some of the profit for yourself

- Owning your own agency, so you can keep some of the sales commissions for yourself

- Utilizing specialty products that will allow you to transform expenses into assets—so you can increase the value of your company for yourself and for your investors

Once you get your own piece of the insurance pie, you can start working on ways to get more out of employees, executives, vendors, and all your professional advisors in the legal, accounting, investment, and insurance industries. Continue to the next section and keep being the giraffe!

CHAPTER 7

The Fifth Secret: Leveraging People— the Advanced Course

"If you do not seek out allies and helpers, then you will be isolated and weak."

—SUN TZU, *The Art of War*

You know from the first secret that your ambitious goals are to reach levels that only one in 100, one in 1,000, or possibly one in 10,000 people ever do. In the second secret, you learned that you can't just work harder. You have to work smarter. You know that you can't do it all yourself. You need to create leverage whenever possible. The single most important, and most powerful, application of leverage is through the efforts of other people.

A quote I like to share is, "The greater the number of people who want to see you succeed, the greater the probability (and level) of your success!" I shared some of the basic building blocks of leveraging people in the second secret. Now we are going to step up our game and take the master's course in leveraging people. You are going to learn ways to get two groups of people to become more engaged and invested in your success. These very important groups are employees and advisors.

Leveraging Employees—Master's Course

First, forget what your employment attorney taught you about the definition of "employees." We are not talking about W-2 employees who qualify for benefits. There is no need to disqualify anybody from your leverage list. Second, embrace the fact that your goal is to maximize leverage. Instead of trying to exclude people from the list to avoid having to pay them benefits, you want to look at this differently. To find a better path to success, you want to include anyone who is affiliated with your business in any way whatsoever. For the purposes of maximizing leverage, our definition of "employees" will include:

1. Employees and executives
2. Independent contractors
3. Partners (in the case of professionals)
4. Investors
5. Board of directors and advisory board members
6. Vendors and suppliers
7. Advertisers and celebrity endorsers
8. Anybody who cashes a check with your name on it!

These are "below the line" items that contribute to the big difference between the top line, or revenue number, and the bottom line, or profit number, on your income statement. How could they be seen as anything other than expenses or debits when they clearly reduce the revenue number? The purpose of *6 Secrets to Leveraging Success* is to help you elevate your perspective so you can see a better path to success. In this section, you will learn how to rethink and restructure how you compensate and motivate these groups of people.

Your success strategy relies on your efficient use of leverage. You know that you need allies to help you. By dismissing the antiquated employment and compensation strategies that worked for workers in the 1950s, you will free your mind to see a better way. By adopting innovative co-investment and partnership strategies with your people, you will create more engaged and more financially motivated people—who will definitely be more interested in seeing you reach your goals. Let's start by exploring strategies that just don't work, so you can stop being part of someone else's plan for success.

Retirement Plans Are for Suckers

Everyone has to have a retirement plan. Without one, people wouldn't ever want to work for you. Here are seven reasons why you should rethink your traditional retirement plan.

Employees Don't Really Want It

How do I know this? Consider one of my good friends and clients, Dr. Andy. Dr. Andy has run a very successful medical practice in Central Texas for 20 years. At any given time, he may have 100 to 120 full-time employees. He pays well and offers very generous benefits, including a 401(k) plan. Over the past 20 years, 200 employees who were previously enrolled in his 401(k) plan have left his employment. Do you want to guess how many of them have rolled over their investment accounts to IRAs? One. Not one guess, one person. Of 200 employees, 199 cashed in their 401(k) right after leaving. None of them was over the age of 59½ at the time. This means that all of them, who were in their prime working years, paid full ordinary income taxes, plus a 10% early-withdrawal penalty, to have access to the money immediately.

Here is a test to see if your employees really want their 401(k) plan. Don't ask your human resources person for an opinion, and don't survey the employees. Every employee would rather have something than not have it. The real test is to ask each employee the following question:

> "Last year, I contributed $1,500 to your 401(k) plan. I am considering a change of plan to give employees a choice. I could continue the plan as it is now or pay you a bonus of $1,200 at the holidays. Which would you choose?"

You likely have employees. Which do you think yours would choose? So far, 100% of my friends and clients surveyed have said,

"Nearly every employee will choose the cash." If we use the example above as a barometer, you could save 20% of your retirement planning dollars *and* have a lot more flexibility—which we will explain in this section.

Executives Can't Utilize Retirement Plans Effectively

First, there are tons of tests. Unless a certain percentage of employees actually participate in the plan, the higher-income owners and executives can't participate. The Department of Labor makes all plans do "top-heavy" testing, to make sure that plans are not favoring the highest earners. The test is solely a participation test. Reasons for not participating are not important. The result is that a company can offer a generous retirement plan, offer to match employees' contributions (which is free money!), and offer to pay all the fees of the plan administration. But if enough employees still don't want to participate, you as the executive or owner still may not be able to contribute to the plan for yourself. What kind of crap is that?

The mutual fund companies are willing to send employees out to many businesses to offer explanations and to conduct enrollment meetings. The purpose of these meetings is to convince the rank-and-file employees to take advantage of the plan so they can see the power of compounded interest work to their benefit. The real reason for the meetings is that the executives can't make their $50,000 annual contributions unless their employees make contributions to satisfy the discriminatory testing required of these plans.

If the executives aren't able to make any contributions to their own retirement accounts, then they aren't going to support and contribute to the plan. If there isn't a plan, then the mutual fund company and retirement plan administrators don't get paid (see point No. 5 below).

Even if you do convince your employees to take responsibility for their own retirement planning and to take advantage of your generous "free money," it still may not be a good plan for you. The maximum contribution for a defined-contribution plan in 2017 is $54,000. This number represents 20% of the maximum allowable salary of $270,000.

This doesn't mean that you can't earn more than $270,000, but any salary above $270,000 is not included for the purposes of calculating allowable contributions. If the executive is over the age of 50, that annual maximum may be increased by the $6,000 catch-up provision, for a total contribution of $60,000.

A classmate of mine in business school, Liz Davidson, wrote an article about the history of retirement plans for the website Workforce. Liz estimated that a person would need to save 11 times his or her pre-tax salary before retirement, to support quality of life after retirement. If you are making $100,000 per year, it's feasible that you could save $1.1 million in a retirement plan. However, if you earn $500,000 per year, it would take outrageous investment returns to turn your $54,000 retirement plan contributions into $5.5 million of savings.

When you are successful, you will need to supplement your retirement plan with additional structures and strategies. Many high-income earners will ultimately utilize more creative plans that offer much larger contributions. My experience is that executives find more tax-efficient plans for themselves, then discontinue their participation in traditional plans. I anticipate this trend to continue as more executives take a closer look at the ineffective plans they currently have.

Retirement Plans Are for Socialists, Not Entrepreneurs

In 1974, the Employee Retirement Income Security Act (ERISA) enacted a combination of federal income tax and labor laws to establish minimum standards for pension plans in private industry. Over 40 years ago, it was very common for an employee to work for an employer for 25 to 40 years and retire with a pension. The very complicated ERISA rules were designed to protect employees in the short term, which would contribute to long-term economic growth.

Unfortunately, the result ended up being something less interesting for business owners. Under ERISA, the retirement plan contributions are based on a percentage of income. A defined-benefit plan factors age into the equation, with older employees generally being able to put away more. There is no ability to alter the contributions based on performance. These particular plans are not meritocracies. Every 43-year-old qualifying employee who earns $50,000 in salary will receive the same retirement plan benefit. Though this may seem fair, it does not help the very ambitious entrepreneur who wants to reward the best and brightest employees, and wants to do so in a way that encourages them to stay with the company long-term. Luckily, there are other ways to accomplish this—which we will discuss later in this section.

Almost a half century later, the Millennial does not intend to work for an employer for ten years, let alone 40. Businesses no longer offer pension plans. Employees are responsible for their own retirement planning, saving, investing, and spending. Few people who are younger than the Baby Boomers even expect Social Security to be around for their benefit when they reach the qualification age—if there will even be one.

Owners Don't Want the Headaches or the Liability of Retirement Plans

You set up a retirement plan to help your employees. You offer them "free money" in the form of matching their contributions. You do this because you want to help them to help themselves. Because you are likely savvier than they are, you assume some important responsibilities by acting on their behalf as the trustee of the retirement plan. For your trouble, you can be sued for:

- Failure to follow the terms of the plan document. You could try to bend the rules to help employees in need, but that may become a serious problem. Even if the employee doesn't complain, the Department of Labor could fine you for not following the plan document—or for not updating it according to changes in employment laws or reporting requirements.

- Lack of diversification. This is a key fiduciary duty. Your job is to help minimize the risk of large investment losses to the plan. Fiduciaries should consider each plan investment as part of the plan's entire portfolio. Fiduciaries need to document their evaluation and investment decisions. Not doing this could lead to litigation or fines.

Compensation Consultants are as Colorful as Beige

Every successful client I have is constantly looking for top talent. These clients have gone through lots of employees and executives in their careers, so they know how important it is to recruit and retain great people. Without them, their leverage is severely stunted. Many of my clients have hired compensation consultants to help them build compensation plans to recruit and retain top talent.

Unfortunately, what business owners really want and what compensation consultants actually offer are completely different. You learned in the first secret, Stop Being Beige, that the most successful don't want to fit in with the crowd. They are always looking for ways to differentiate themselves from others in their industry. However, compensation consultants specialize in the averages and ranges of compensation and benefits packages for specific industries.

If your company offers a cultural or non-financial incentive that is a truly extraordinary differentiator, and people would work for you for less money, then a compensation consultant can tell you what others are paying so you can target your financial compensation to be a little lower. If your company is like almost every company and your talent wants to get paid well to work for you, then you may want to talk to compensation consultants to see what not to do to differentiate your company to the more creative and highest-performing talent. Otherwise, save yourself the money and don't waste your time hiring a compensation consultant.

Retirement Plans are 70% Tax Traps!

If you are reading this book, you are undoubtedly planning to have a net worth above the estate tax exemption. As of 2017, the unified exemption amount is $5.49 million. You may leave this amount during your lifetime, or at death, with no estate tax liability. Most investors are shocked to find out that 70% to 80% of the assets left in a retirement plan at death will end up with state and federal tax agencies. If the highest marginal income tax rates are 43% to 52%, you may be scratching your head as to how this is even possible.

This is because of the unusual tax treatment of something called IRD, which stands for *income in respect of a decedent*. These are dollars that would have been taxable to the decedent (person who died) had the decedent lived long enough to receive the income. IRD includes unpaid bonuses or royalty payments, as well as retirement plan assets, such as pensions, 401(k) plans and IRAs. These assets are essentially worth nothing to your children.

To oversimplify, IRD is included in the taxable estate of the person who has passed away. This means it could generate a 40% estate tax liability. In addition, the heirs who inherit the retirement plan will still have to pay ordinary income taxes on any distributions. The odd thing is that you do not get full credit for one against the other. The result: each retirement plan dollar is worth 20 to 30 cents to your children. There are three solutions to this problem:

1. Don't contribute to inflexible retirement plans.
2. Start spending down your retirement plans at age 59½ try to spend all the money before you die (though it's tough to predict perfectly).
3. Leave it to charity or a family foundation when you die (described in detail in the sixth secret).

You're a Muppet for the Mutual Fund Companies

Please indulge me for a little context. In March 2012, Greg Smith resigned from Goldman Sachs. The former executive director and vice president went out with a bang—penning an op-ed in *The New York Times* in which he called Goldman's culture "toxic and destructive." Smith's letter came during a devastating financial crisis. Goldman had emerged as the rich and arrogant perpetrator of financial wreckage that left many hardworking Americans holding the proverbial bag. Smith made a now infamous reference to Muppets: "I have seen five different managing directors refer to their own clients as 'Muppets,' sometimes over internal e-mail."

First, the Muppet reference is to Jim Henson's television show. Kermit the Frog, Miss Piggy, and Gonzo were just three of the puppet characters created by Henson. Second, the Goldman Sachs reference has nothing to do with comedy and everything to do with puppets. My take on Smith's commentary is that Goldman's clients acted as if the firm was pulling the strings. Somehow, when the housing market crashed, investors lost money in their mortgage-backed securities and Goldman made billions. There is a very interesting commentary about this in two documentaries, *The Inside Job* and *The Big Short*. You can form your own conclusion. For now, keep this story in mind as you read about mutual fund companies.

Mutual fund assets held in retirement accounts (IRAs and defined-contribution plans), including 401(k) plans, stood at $8 trillion as of the end of March 2017 (source: Investment Company Institute, ICI. org). That amount means 47% of all mutual fund assets are held by retirement plans. Eight trillion dollars! You may ask, why is size a bad thing? I am going to tell you.

You have undoubtedly heard the quote, "It's what you don't know that is going to kill you." The enormous retirement plan industry has fees that are a secret to most people. *Kiplinger* quoted an AARP survey in which 80% of people surveyed had no idea how much they paid in fees for their retirement plans. The lack of transparency is a problem that *Bloomberg* tried to tackle in an article dated August 23, 2017. Bloomberg quoted an NEPC investigation of 123 retirement plans. These plans represented $138 billion in total invested assets, and the average expense fee for these plans was found to be 0.41%. This was in addition to an average record-keeping fee of $59 per person per year. But wait! These fees are in addition to the fees for the actual mutual funds themselves.

You can invest in a Vanguard index fund and pay 0.04% in fees. Or, you can invest in the same Vanguard fund inside your retirement plan and pay $59 per year plus 0.44% in expenses. I'm too frustrated with the whole industry to dive down a rabbit hole and calculate how much these crazy fees will decimate your retirement. Trust me that the most successful people don't bother with retirement plans in their planning.

> **"I would rather gamble on our vision than on a 'me too' product."**
>
> —STEVE JOBS

Don't think about a retirement plan the way the mutual fund companies want you to think about it—as a necessity. Ask yourself if your planning is helping your employees to help themselves? Is it making them happy? Is it helping your business attract and retain the top talent you need to reach your goals? Or, is your current benefits plan just boring—or beige? Before you just approve another antiquated strategy because it is part of the way things have always been done, think about what you are trying to accomplish. Then ask yourself if what you are about to do is actually helping you reach your goals. If not, maybe it's time to consider taking a different path.

Phantom Stock, Deferred Compensation, and Stock Options Are Tax Disasters

Something I have heard many culture consultants and entrepreneurs talk about is "getting employees to act like owners." One way to do that is to give every single employee a good deal of stock. You could create an employee stock ownership plan (ESOP), but that would require you to give up a lot of equity, and it might have the same socialist vibe we discussed earlier. To try to give the illusion of ownership, many companies offer phantom stock, deferred compensation, or stock options.

The big problem for the employee is the tax liability. The owner has all the control—if, when, and how the company will be sold. The employees can't really plan for the event, but they get stuck with ordinary income tax when their phantom stock vests. Deferred compensation is always taxable to the participants. An event that gives the employee "constructive receipt" can trigger a huge tax liability. Stock options? I have a degree in applied mathematics, am a Certified Financial Planner professional, and have worked in taxation and business building for 20 years. I still find the timing and taxation of incentive stock options confusing. And if you exercise your options and then the stock price drops between your election date and the date you plan to sell the options (one year later hoping for long-term capital gains treatment), you can have a tax liability on stock value you never received. It happened a lot in the early 2000s.

Unfunded Defined-Benefit Plans May Topple Law Firms and CPA Firms

ERISA was created to protect employees and their pensions in private industry. Lawyers and accountants are exempt. Though freedom and flexibility are generally outstanding characteristics, I need to remind you of the idiom that begins, "Give a man enough rope." It appears that many professional partnerships are on the verge of hanging themselves.

The retirement plan for many professional firms is to pay partners some amount of money after they have been with the firm for some period of time. It might be the average of the partner's last five years' production paid each year for five years after he or she works for the firm for 20 years. There are many variations. According to an anonymous source at Wells Fargo (which banks more than three-fourths of the Am Law 100 law firms), approximately 80% of the company's clients have unfunded defined-benefit plans. We have met with law firms whose mergers (which were already announced) ultimately did not go through because one firm had future liabilities to partners totaling over $200 million (and the merging partner had no such liability). At least one of the Big 4 accounting firms has an unfunded plan of over $2 billion.

I know that these firms are looking for answers to these problems. I also know that they are fearful that their star attorneys and accountants who are in their 40s and 50s are not interested in forgoing a decade or more of bonuses so the firm can pay off its partners who are in their 60s and 70s. I predict that many young guns will leave the firms that have made big promises to senior partners, and will either start their own firms or join firms that don't have these problems. I am making this prediction because I run a small consulting firm that can help only three or four big firms per year with big unfunded liabilities. Something has to give.

> **"When people are financially invested, they want a return. When people are emotionally invested, they want to contribute."**
>
> —SIMON SINEK

The Solution: Invest *with* Employees

As the business owner, you want to inspire your people to act like owners. You know you can't sustain it with lots of "rah-rah." You know you can't afford to just dole out lots of moolah. You're looking for that moment of *aha*!

You have to find a way to put your employees in a position where they benefit when you benefit. For Millennials who want to feel like they are wanted, you must make them understand how they are vital contributors to your future success. If you can let go of all those other strategies that others want you to use (for their benefit, maybe?), and you can elevate your perspective, you might just see this new, better path to success. I call it TrEE.

The TrEE Program Transforms Expenses Into Equity

What kind of expenses? Most successful businesses inefficiently utilize valuable capital for incentive compensation, bonuses, employee and executive benefits, deferred compensation, and incentive stock options. While your company may be wasting valuable resources on the aforementioned items, you are also spending valuable time and money on interest payments (if you have debt), compliance reporting and meetings (with lenders), shareholder communications, capital raising (if you need additional capital), shareholder dividends, executive recruiters, new-hire training and onboarding, and retirement plan onboarding, among other items.

How much employee and executive time and company money are spent on all of those areas I just listed? One million dollars? Ten million? A hundred million? The larger your company, the more you are wasting in those areas. Imagine if we could redeploy the capital in the first list so that your employees could replace much of your need for outside investors, bank financing, and all the unnecessary reporting and aggravation that go with it. If you didn't have to worry about shareholders and banking covenants, how much more efficient would your people be? How much more profitable would your company be?

If your employees were all participating in the savings and in the excess value creation, would you ever need to pay a recruiter again? Or, would you have the greatest workforce on the planet? Is a 401(k) giving you that kind of return? Are you getting this type of great idea from Fidelity or Deloitte or Northwestern Mutual? Not a chance. I'm not picking on those companies. There isn't a mutual fund company, an accounting firm, or an insurance company coming up with a groundbreaking strategy like TrEE. I know because I have worked with a number of them to try to help them implement plans like this one. They are so in love with their own product lines and their processes that they don't want to hear the truth about what business owners need. They just can't handle the truth.

How Does TrEE Work?

In *Mastering the Art of Success*, I wrote a section called "Increasing Sales Without Ever Selling." One of the strategies I shared was to partner with your clients. TrEE is a partnership in the truest sense. It is a partnership between the company, the employees, and the investors. By eliminating all of those wasted expenses, the company will significantly increase its earnings. The increased earnings will increase the value of the company—how much the company increases its value will depend on the price-to-earnings (P/E) ratio or the multiple (of earnings) that is ultimately paid at sale. Everyone, other than the future buyers, will benefit from higher earnings.

In anticipation of fantastic future growth and increased profitability, the company will invest its profits with its employees. That's right! Instead of getting employees to reinvest their tax-inefficient retirement plan dollars back into the company (like employees at Enron did), the company will take its dollars that are taxed at a potentially lower corporate tax rate and invest them with employees. These investments will be done at arm's-length rates per Internal Revenue Code guidance. Right now, those rates are less than 3%. That rate will be locked in for the remainder of the employee's lifetime. The employee gets all of the investment value during his or her lifetime. The company will not receive any piece of the employee's investment until the employee dies.

Employees will be able to direct the investment of the proceeds from the employer into a range of investments that fit their individual risk tolerances. One of the investments will be life insurance. This investment may be 10% to 30% of the total investment from the employee—depending on the age and health of the employee. That life insurance will protect the employee's family from any unfortunate premature death. The life insurance will also ensure that the company gets repaid for its investment at the death of the employee.

How Is TrEE Better Than Deferred Compensation?

The TrEE investment from the company into the account for the employee is not taxable to the employee. Deferred compensation is taxed at ordinary income tax rates. TrEE is a separate account, not subject to creditors of the company. Deferred compensation benefits could be seized by a creditor of the company. TrEE gives the employees access to and control of funds right away. Deferred compensation is not available to the employee for use or control. Deferred compensation is a liability to the company. When it is paid, it is an expense to the company, lowering its earnings. TrEE is an asset to the company. It improves the value of the company and will enhance the value at the time of sale.

In our experience, incentive compensation, stock options, and bonuses that get restructured as TrEE benefits create a 50% to 75% increase in after-tax benefits to the employees. That value is in addition to the significant benefit that TrEE affords the sponsoring company. If a company redeploys $10 million of bonuses or incentive compensation in a given year, and that company has a P/E ratio of 15, the company's total value will increase by $150 million for the shareholders. If your company is in a lower-growth industry and you someday sell for six times earnings, the owners will get $60 million more for the sale of the company. In what other area can you do something great for your employees *and* create massive value for the owners at the same time?

Who Is the Best Candidate for TrEE?

TrEE can be altered to fit the specific needs of the sponsoring company. It works particularly well for:

- Not-for-profit institutions
- Universities (for presidents, coaches, highly paid staff, or researchers)
- Companies with retained earnings
- Companies with net operating losses (NOLs)
- Companies with loss carryforwards
- Companies with large amounts of depreciable equipment
- Organizations where unreasonable executive compensation is bad publicity
- Healthcare companies that pay physicians (directly or indirectly)
- Private-equity-owned portfolio companies

- Family-owned businesses that want to transfer wealth to future generations
- Companies with highly paid boards of directors
- Companies that want to sell in the next three years
- Publicly traded companies with high P/E ratios
- Companies that have below-expected earnings
- Turnaround and leveraged buyout (LBO) situations
- CPA firms with unfunded defined-benefit plans
- Law firms with unfunded defined-benefit plans
- Companies that pays celebrity or athlete endorsers
- Companies in the entertainment industry (film, television, professional sports)
- Any firm that pays talent millions of dollars per year
- Any company that pays royalties (publishing, film, television, music)

This is a rather flexible structure that works well in various circumstances. The design of the plan will vary significantly from one client to another. One application of the program has been favorably reviewed by the head of global tax at one of the Big 4 accounting firms. These are the most fun projects we handle at JarvisTower, so this is the only shameless plug I will put in the book. If you are interested in seeing how TrEE might work for you or for one of your clients, find us www.JarvisTower.com or call me at 817-442-6006.

Leveraging Advisors—Master's Course

Increased success leads to increased complexity. Once you reach a certain level of success, you turn your attention from exclusively asking, "How can I make more money?" to letting other questions share the spotlight, including:

1. What happens if I get sued?
2. Where can I find cheaper money to fuel my company's growth?
3. How do I pay less tax?
4. How, when, where, and at what price will I be able to sell my company?
5. How do I know what insurance I really need?
6. What kind of incentive plan will help me keep my best people?
7. Where do I invest all my money?
8. Who will give me advice that isn't self-serving?

> **"Never underestimate the power of stupid people in large groups."**
>
> —GEORGE CARLIN

You can find experts in a specific field to help you answer each of these questions. The problem arises when you attempt to answer the next question. You will look for another specialist to answer that question. This process will repeat itself indefinitely. You may be in the middle of this vicious cycle right now.

Today there is increased regulation in all areas of finance and professional services. Every industry and government agency seems to have increased its regulations. General counsel and human resources executives have a heightened sensitivity to political correctness, bad publicity, and potential litigation. As a result, we have become a society of sub-sub-specialists. Each person is an expert in a very specific area.

There are no more generalists who have a great appreciation for all of the elements of your plan. Even if there are some Renaissance men at one of the firms you have hired, they are likely to be forbidden from speaking about things the firm's errors and omissions policy doesn't cover. It shouldn't surprise you that the firm's errors and omissions policy covers only products or services that the firm sells. Where does this leave you? In a Catch-22, I'm afraid.

Having a team of sub-specialists working in their own silos is like starting an orchestra without a conductor and without letting the musicians practice together. You can't just put a bunch of great musicians together with no sheet music, no guidance, and no discussion, and expect them to do something perfectly the first time. Unfortunately, this is what happens with almost every client I meet. There is a better way.

Identify Potential Conflicts

Imagine a world where all of your advisors are looking for ways to help you to increase your income, reduce your expenses, and take things off your plate. Imagine that the advisors are working together to accomplish your goal, not working independently for their own individual goals. Imagine that instead of seeing invoice after painful invoice from your advisors, you actually make money from this group while getting valuable advice and achieving additional leverage. This may sound like Shangri-La, but it doesn't have to be your lost horizon. This is what you are going to learn how to do right now.

Earlier, you learned to include many different people in your "employee" group when you were looking for better ways to leverage their time, their intellect, their creativity, and their passion. Now, you will learn how to set better conditions and clearer expectations for your advisory team.

Advisors you should leverage, not pay:

- Accountants
- Attorneys
- Insurance agents and brokers
- Investment advisors
- Financial planners

Accountants

The term "accountant" will be used to generically describe an accountant, a Certified Public Accountant (CPA), or an enrolled agent (EA). What they do: accountants are trained and licensed to prepare tax returns for submission to the IRS. Each state has its own licensing and accreditation procedures for accountants and CPAs. In the most desirable client-advisor relationship, the accountants also provide clients with advice on tax matters. Accountants generally bill by the hour.

Potential Conflict: Bigger Is Not Always Better

In 2016, I had a meeting with some people in the private client group of a Big 4 firm. They told me that their group was forbidden from discussing advanced strategies with its CEO and high-net-worth clients. The reason they gave me was that the powers that be in the organization didn't want an overzealous IRS agent to attack the firm for its "aggressive" tax planning. The bad press could threaten the firm's very profitable audit practice. They suggested that a better outcome would be for their high-income executives to hire me for planning and then go back to the Big 4 firm for the accounting and compliance associated with the strategies. It may sound totally absurd, but it is 100% true.

Attorneys

The term "attorney" describes someone admitted to the bar association in the state(s) in which he or she wishes to practice. You may have a number of attorneys who specialize in corporate issues, litigation, asset protection, estate planning, income tax, or dozens of other specialties. They generally charge by the hour, but some flat-fee work is possible.

Potential Conflict: To Fee or Not to Fee

The attorney situation is similar to the accounting conflict. There are so many different specialties that one attorney, or even one firm, may struggle to help you in all areas of need. Since there is very little recurring revenue for attorneys from clients, new engagements must be generated annually. This may create an incentive for attorneys to either extend the work or to refer you to their colleagues.

Insurance Agents and Brokers

Insurance agents and brokers provide various types of insurance policies to clients. Some insurance professionals also offer financial planning or investment solutions. Insurance agents and brokers must have a resident agent license in the state in which they reside. Certified Financial Planners, accountants, investment advisors, and attorneys can all secure life insurance licenses.

Potential Conflict: They Don't Work for You

Follow the money. You pay the insurance company a premium for your insurance product. The insurance companies pay the insurance agents commissions for their sales of products. You don't generally pay the insurance agent anything. Some agents are restricted, or heavily incented, to sell the products of one company (Northwestern Mutual, New York Life, Mass Mutual, and so on) because they have a heavily subsidized career agent contract. Other independent agents have the freedom to sell the products of any company, but almost every agent is part of some affinity group or organization that offers additional support, awards, or other incentives to sell their products.

Though it is not required by law (yet) for agents to disclose commissions, I highly suggest that you ask your agent or broker to tell you exactly what he or she makes in hard (direct) and soft (indirect) payments for selling you the policy. If you are afraid to tell your client how you get paid and how much you get paid for the service you are providing, then maybe there is something wrong with this relationship. Insurance plays a huge role in the planning for most of my clients. It's a shame that the shady sales practices of some less morally directed salespeople give the industry a bad name. Note: before you accuse me of bashing the industry, you should know that I have been one of the top insurance agents in the country for the better part of 15 years and have won top agent honors (out of 14,000 agents licensed to work with that particular company) in two separate years. This is because I create partnerships with my clients (see the fourth secret for a few ideas on that).

Investment Advisors

I use the term "investment advisor" to include money managers, stockbrokers, private client service groups, private bankers, and private wealth advisor—and we might even be able to throw private equity firms into this "private" group. These advisors have to study and pass a three-hour securities exam and a 90-minute ethics exam or file as an independent registered investment advisor directly with the US Securities and Exchange Commission. Investment advisors handle investments for clients. They typically take a fee based on the amount of assets they manage. Some have incentive-based compensation as well. Few consider taxes.

Limitation

Most focus on gross, pre-tax returns and fail to adequately manage taxes. The majority of investments may belong to pensions, endowments, or other corporate accounts—which are less sensitive to taxation than the personal holdings of the most successful families.

Potential Conflict: It's Always a Good Time to Buy

Investment advisors are paid based on the assets under management (AUM). The more money they invest for their clients, the more money they earn for the firm and for themselves. Many of my colleagues and I joke that there are only two stories you get from your investment advisor:

- The market is up. You want to stay in the market and ride out this wave.
- The market is down. It's a great time to buy!

It's absolutely amazing. The people who get paid to manage money always think it's a good time for you to put more money in the market, and that it's never a good time to sell and take your money out of the market altogether.

Financial Planners

I use the term "financial planner" to describe someone who charges a fee to create a financial plan for a client. Sometimes this is a Certified Financial Planner, who has taken six courses over a number of years, met an ethics standard, and passed a much more rigorous exam than the other financial and insurance professionals. (I have passed them all; the CFP is by far the hardest.) The biggest difference between Certified Financial Planners and other insurance-related advisors is that CFPs actually have a fiduciary relationship. This means they have to put your interests ahead of theirs. Insurance agents only have to meet a suitability standard. As long as they aren't hurting you, it is okay if the planning is better for them than for you. Someone with a CFP designation could not do that while complying with the organization's code of ethics.

Potential Conflict: Wolf in Sheep's Clothing?

The financial planner can be a salesperson in disguise. It can be hard to distinguish between the true planner and the disguised salesperson, ultimately focused on selling insurance products or investment management services. You may have to ask a few questions to find out what the real motivations are for the planner. You may also, when hiring the planner, suggest that you want a 100% unbiased person to do the planning and that you may use someone else for the products. Ask the planner to quote you a fee assuming that you would not use him or her for any implementation. It may help you figure out the motivations if they are unclear.

You now know a little more about each discipline that may be represented on your team. Before you learn to create more efficient working relationships with the people in those disciplines, you need to make sure you have the right team.

Measure Twice, Cut Once

In the bestselling book *Good to Great: Why Some Companies Make the Leap and Others Don't*, Jim Collins talks about "getting the right people on the bus." Let's take a quick inventory to see if you have any warning signs of underperforming advisory groups.

Warning Signs of Inefficient Advisory Boards

- You have had the same advisors for many years
- You don't interview potential replacement advisors for new ideas
- Your advisors don't bring you new recommendations regularly
- Your advisors reject ideas you bring to them without offering detailed explanations
- Your advisors are too familiar with each other, and they don't challenge each other
- You rarely, if ever, have paid for second opinions from other professionals
- Your advisory team does not meet regularly to coordinate your planning
- You feel guilty when you consider replacing one of your advisors

Do any of these warning signs hit close to home? If so, you may need some new blood on your advisory team. Before you rush out and hire your friends, your partner's advisor, or your golf buddy, please take a couple of minutes to read *Seven Ways Not to Hire Advisors* (see the Additional Resources section). You may want to hire an organizational development person to help you find advisory board members who not only have different areas of expertise, but also have different personality strengths that will supplement your style. A healthy balance of experiences, ages, and personalities is a great recipe for success in any group.

Your advisory team may be almost as important to you and your family as your executive and management teams are to your business. By taking a more structured and scientific approach to building this team correctly from the start, you will likely

> **"The people have the power. All we have to do is awaken the power in the people."**
>
> —JOHN LENNON

save yourself valuable time, preserve a valuable friendship or two, and reach your goals faster and with fewer headaches. Once you have your group of core advisors from multiple disciplines, it's time to help them to help you (cue Tom Cruise and Cuba Gooding Jr. in *Jerry Maguire*).

Set Them Up for Success

Are you amazed when you see a news story about some fool who was mauled by a pet tiger or alligator, or some other exotic pet? Of course, you're not. Animals will ultimately behave like animals. Am I suggesting that all advisors are animals? Maybe.

When we get busy, overwhelmed, or stressed, we all subconsciously revert to who we really are. Jack Welch, the legendary CEO of General Electric, famously took all potential executive hires out for a round of golf. He wanted to see how people handled adversity before he hired them, believing it's hard to hide your character when you play golf. This applies not only to personality traits but to training as well. We all get busy and we all face challenges. When that happens, advisory board members will do what they are trained to do. Attorneys will identify risks. Accountants will organize. Salespeople will sell. Managers will manage. Leaders will lead.

You must set the rules of engagement and create structures that will leverage each advisor's unique combination of personality, skills, and experience for *your benefit*. Now that we have identified the limitations of each category of advisor, let's dig into some practical steps you can take to make your advisors work better for you.

Paid Board Meetings

Over a decade ago, I met with the partners of The Founders Group in San Diego. They deal only with families with a net worth greater than $25 million. This group found that the most efficient families arranged semi-annual, all-day (or multiple-day) meetings with all of their advisors and family members. The costs of flying in advisors to participate in these meetings and paying them their hourly wages can total $50,000 to $100,000 per year.

According to Joe Strazzeri of The Founders Group, "The families that make this effort to spend time with the experts on their team generally see these meetings as the family's most productive use of time and money spent throughout the year."

As with any collaborative endeavor, the collection of people is not enough to Insure Success. Every conference call and meeting must have an agenda and someone to manage the meeting to make sure that all the important items are handled in the allotted time. It is common to put one of the advisors in charge of organizing and facilitating information flow among the other advisors. This is usually a financial planner, but personalities will dictate roles. Within the group, you need to identify roles and responsibilities and make one person accountable for the completion of each task.

When considering different options, it is wonderful when there is a unanimous decision on whether or not to go in a particular direction. However, many decisions will not be unanimous. You need to establish the percentage for approvals (simple majority, two-thirds majority, or 80% super majority, as examples) concerning how decisions are to be made within the group and share them with the group. If the people involved know how you are going to make decisions, it will make it easier for them to participate in the group and allow them to continue to participate even when the rest of the group disagrees with a particular decision.

The Family Office Concept

Simply put, a family office is a legal entity created for the purpose of treating the family's wealth as a business. Some advisors recommend participating in a multi-family office (serving a number of families) when wealth exceeds $50 million. Single-family offices are advised at either the $100 million or $250 million threshold. A wealth-management-focused family office may perform centralized management or oversight of investments, tax planning, estate planning, and philanthropic planning. A more comprehensive family office may provide tax compliance work, secure access to private banking and private trust services, manage documents and recordkeeping, handle expenses and bill paying, keep the books, educate family members on finance, provide family support services, and offer family governance.

The most significant difference between a formal family office and an informal set of advisors who work for a wealthy family is in compensation. With a formal family office, the advisors actually work for the family. The advisors often include accountants, attorneys, investment advisors, and financial planners. The professional employees receive a salary and possibly a bonus or "carry" on certain investments or projects. There are usually no billable hours or commissions. This allows the family to accomplish three things:

1. Ensure that advisors are giving the family its undivided attention;
2. Align interests and eliminate potential conflicts; and
3. Manage, or smooth out, expenses by eliminating large invoices.

You may not wish to go all-in on the family office for your family, but you may want to borrow some of the pieces of the model. You could buy a block of time from your accountant, attorney, and investment advisor with the expressed intent that you are going to get them to work for you during that time and that anything they do during that time will not be subject to additional billing. By pre-purchasing a certain number of hours, you may get a better rate than if you were subject to hour-by-hour billing. You may also structure the payment to the professionals as board of directors' compensation. Your advisors' firms may be more flexible with a board of directors-type arrangement than with reduced billable hours. Each situation is different.

Self-Insured Family

Historically, insurance brokerage is not included in the family office. I am trying to change that, as our firm is implementing insurance brokerage arrangements for a number of our most successful families. In the fourth secret, Insure Success, we talked about the value of vertically integrating your business's benefits, human resources, and risk management departments to include insurance brokerage and agency revenues. By creating a joint venture with an independent insurance agent or agency, you can eliminate that major conflict of interest with the commission-based insurance agent. By owning a company together, you create full transparency of the revenues.

Most interesting to our clients who consider this model is that the creation of a partnership creates a fiduciary duty between our clients and our firm. Usually, insurance agents are held to a suitability standard (which is a much lower level of care). By creating a legal, fiduciary relationship between us and our clients, we eliminate the fear that the insurance agent or broker is going to do something that is in his or her best interest and at the expense of the client. I am proud to say that this is one of my favorite "giraffe" strategies. While everyone else is trying to fight commission disclosure legislation to protect the secrecy of commissions, we are creating ways of making the insurance process fully transparent. While all clients fear how an insurance agent might be screwing them, we are creating an arrangement in which we give our clients a higher standard of care and share the revenues with them. We give more and get paid less. Who doesn't like the idea of better service and lower costs?

See a Better Path

"If you want to go fast, go alone. If you want to go far, go together." That is a famous African proverb. The people who work for your company and with your company are closest to your main wealth driver. You need to find a way to get as many of them as possible committed to your vision of success. By offering the same benefits as every other company, you are being beige. Stop doing things that other people want you to do. Don't feed the mutual funds beast and be part of their success story. Don't give in to the human resources person who may be uncomfortable with change. Get away from the 401(k) and don't waste your time with phantom stock or deferred compensation tax traps.

This is your company. This is your ambitious definition of success. You know you have to be different. Try to be different in as many areas as you can. People will be the biggest leverage you can ever utilize. Adopt an innovative approach to working with your employees, your investors, your vendors, and your strategic partners. Whether you utilize our TrEE plan to transform employee and executive expense into equity or you find a new way to connect with your people, do something differently.

Seriously consider the use of a paid advisory board. Make it a priority to get the right people on your bus. Look for people who have personality tests to prove that they are innovative, creative disruptors. You want people who think differently to help you elevate your perspective. Once you have the right people, create structures where your advisors will no longer be an expense to you and your business. Get them to become your partners in your nouveau family office structure so you can eliminate conflicts of interest and trust that everyone is rowing the boat in the same direction as you are.

I am confident that you are on your way to reaching your ambitious goals, but there is one step left. Becoming a success does not guarantee that you will pass those traits down to your children and grandchildren. There is a powerful quote, "Show me the son of a wealthy father. He will not become the father of a wealthy son." If you want your business, your family, and your legacy to continue past your life, there are many valuable lessons for you. Please continue to the sixth secret to learn why the chapter is titled, "Be a Legend—Leave a Legacy."

CHAPTER 8

The Sixth Secret: Be a Legend— Leave a Legacy

"If a man is proud of his wealth, he should not be praised until it is known how he employs it."

—SOCRATES

In the beginning of the book, you set some very ambitious goals. At that time, I asked only what your goals were. I then focused on helping you adjust your mindset so you could be better prepared for the challenges ahead of you. Once you understood and appreciated the difficulty of the undertaking, and you put yourself in the right frame of mind to be able to reach such a high level of success, I offered practical business and personal planning strategies to help achieve your goals more quickly and efficiently. Now I must ask you the single most important question about the very ambitious goals you have set for yourself, your company, and your family.

Why?

Why did you set your goals so high? Why are you working so hard? Why are you willing to take so many chances? Why do you want to leverage your success beyond what you already had before you picked up my book?

I must credit my dear friend Chris Erblich for asking me the "why" question when I was struggling with writer's block on this book. It was so memorable an experience that I remember where I was, what I was doing, and whom I was with at the time. I was in Orlando, Florida, with my wife Heather, walking through a model home, during a relentless thunderstorm. I don't have a Clue whether I was in the study or the kitchen, but I do distinctly remember a candlestick.

Chris Erblich is a lot of things—devoted family man, avid reader, crazy St. Louis Cardinals fan, and creative problem solver. Chris is also a very successful trust and estate attorney who works with many billionaire families. Chris only asked me the same question he asks all of his clients. Why? Why did I want to write another book? Why would this book be seen differently from the many I had written before it? Why was I struggling to get it done? This question had the same impact on me that it has on so many of his clients who, despite accumulating enormous wealth, never got around to finalizing their estate planning. The question made me think. The thinking made me feel. The feelings made me act. Now it's your turn!

What's Your "Why?"

Something motivates you. Perhaps you grew up very poor and you went without as a child. You may want to make sure your grandchildren, great-grandchildren, and generations beyond that never have to struggle to pay for healthcare or education. Maybe you are on a crusade to find a cure for cancer, to feed the hungry, or to provide shelter for the homeless. You may be unselfishly and thanklessly trying to save the whales or another endangered species from extinction. You could be striving to bring peace to a war-torn region. You may be trying to help give every human being on the planet an equal chance for life, liberty, and the pursuit of happiness.

My life's mission is to improve the lives of 1 million children while being a great role model for my three. I graciously accept positions on a few charitable or educational boards each year in an attempt to reach more people. I build programs for nonprofit organizations to increase their endowments so they can help more people and find more effective ways to communicate their missions.

I don't share my "why" to impress you. I share it to impress upon you that the idea of leverage is key to one's legacy. You have busted your ass. With your more ambitious goals, you are going to have to push even harder. You must be doing it for some reason. I can't imagine that you want to beat the odds, achieve a level of success so very few ever will, then see it all get squandered away on fancy cars, jewelry, and ex-spouses.

Take a few minutes and think about it now. How would you like the wealth you create during your lifetime to be distributed after you pass away?

TABLE 13: How Should Your Wealth Be Distributed Upon Your Death?

%	Amount	Recipients
____%	$ _____	A) Children, grandchildren, future generations
____%	$ _____	B) Charities (specify: _____)
____%	$ _____	C) State and federal tax agencies
100%	$ _____	

The following pages will help you more efficiently reach the financial goals you wrote or imagined in the blanks. Some combination of these ideas will supplement the basic estate planning (wills, living trusts, irrevocable life insurance trusts, powers of attorney, LLCs, etc.). If you have not done these important steps yet and you want to learn the estate planning secrets of the affluent, go to www.jarvistower.com/resources. When you subscribe to the free newsletter, you'll gain access to many free downloads, including estate planning excerpts from my previous books.

Category A: Leave It to Heirs

Maybe you sacrificed yourself and did it all for your family. Perhaps you worked really hard for your entire life and you weren't around as much as you would have liked to be. Now you want to leave your loved ones something. Maybe you don't have a charity or university that you think is worthy of your millions, so the kids or grandkids win by process of elimination. Now that you have determined how much you want to leave to your heirs, I no longer care about the why. My job is to show you how to leave more money to your heirs with less aggravation, less tax friction, and less chance of their losing it or wasting it.

Strategy No. 1: The $11 Million "Genie in a Bottle"

I asked my daughters, Chloe and Kierstin, what three things they would wish for if I gave them $11 million. My prudent twelve-year-old first said, "I'd wish for infinite wishes"—always one smart-ass in the crowd. When I called her greedy and said she wouldn't get any money, she prudently said, "I'd want to keep it safe so nobody could take it." My more adventurous nine-year-old added, "It has to be someplace where we can get it when we want it." My eavesdropping son, Tyler (fifteen), pays a lot of attention to my business dealings. He is fascinated by who some of my clients are. He threw in his two cents from the other room: "Don't forget about all the taxes!" My three young kids came up with the three things we all want: access to the money, asset protection, and tax exemption. This is exactly what the "his-and-hers trusts" strategy offers.

His-and-her trusts are the second-greatest estate planning development in the past twenty years (the best will come later). Forget the outdated idea of a marriage penalty in the tax code. This is a strategy that every couple should use, and it almost makes up for all those years of extra income tax payments. I was taught this strategy by my four favorite estate planning attorneys: Chris Erblich in Phoenix, Gal Kaufman in Washington, DC, Ken Vanway in Austin, and David York in Salt Lake City. With apologies to all four of them, I will attempt to oversimplify how it works:

1. Each person in the couple signs a separate property agreement. Husband takes at least $5.5 million of assets. Wife takes at least $5.5 million of assets.
2. Husband gifts his $5.5 million to a trust for the benefit of his wife and their kids. Wife is the trustee in charge of the trust administration and management.
3. Wife gifts her $5.5 million to a trust for the benefit of her husband, their kids and their (current and unborn) grandchildren. Husband is the trustee in charge of the trust administration and management.
4. Both trusts are set up with generation-skipping language that allows funds to pass down to the next generation(s) without any gift or estate tax.
5. All funds in both trusts are available to either the husband or the wife.
6. All funds are protected from creditors of the trustees and beneficiaries.
7. All funds pass down to the children tax-free.
8. One trust asset may pass all the way down to grandchildren tax-free.
9. If the estate tax exemption goes up, the couple can make additional gifts.
10. If the estate tax exemption is lowered or eliminated altogether, the gifts are (more than likely) grandfathered.

Where's the Genie?

The husband and wife each control $5.5 million in their respective trusts. Together, they have access to and control of all $11 million. The funds are held in trust, protected from creditors. Any unspent dollars in the trusts will pass to their children tax-free—and will remain protected from the kids' potential ex-spouses as well.

The total cost for this strategy may be between $10,000 and $25,000 for the two trusts and the separate property agreement. The exact cost is determined by the type of assets, the location of the firm (New

York is not New Mexico), and the complexity of the asset protection language in the trust documents. This is a drop in the bucket relative to the $11 million that will be protected. It's likely to be the biggest bang for the buck that you will get for an estate valued at $25 million or less.

Strategy No. 2: Build Inside the Sanctuary

If you are going to build a financial empire while reaching your new goals, you want to do so within a new, completely safe (from taxes and lawsuits) environment. This strategy works best if you have a living parent or relative. My father offered to make a small gift to me a couple of years ago. My dear friend Ken Vanway suggested that my father create a beneficiary defective trust for me (and my family). The idea was that my father could make a gift to the trust, instead of to me. I thought the gift was too small; Ken took me to school to teach me a valuable lesson. I used a few thousand dollars in that trust to capitalize JarvisTower.

This is my consulting firm that does very large engagements for multi-national firms. This same firm is a licensed insurance agency that generates over a million dollars per year in institutional transactions. With a small capitalization amount, I was able to start a business that would be directed by me (as the trustee of my trust), remain protected from creditors, and grow outside my taxable estate. The cool part of this structure is that the tax bill comes to me. More traditional grantor trusts send the tax liability back to the person who created the trust. I don't want my father to get my tax bill and have a heart attack. This is the best piece of planning I've ever done.

Strategy No. 3: Stay at a Hilton; Don't Raise Your Daughter Like One

It may be unfair of me to badmouth someone I have never met. There may or may not be a famous heir to a rather significant family fortune who is best known for her party-girl reputation. The point I am making is that you don't want to leave money to your children in a way that stunts their work ethic or that causes them to make irresponsible choices. Put another way, you want the legacy you leave to have a positive impact on your family and on the greater community.

> **"Rich men's sons are seldom rich men's fathers."**
>
> —HERBERT KAUFMAN

There are a number of ways that you can structure the terms of the inheritance to promote more responsible behavior and to encourage the ideals that you espouse. You can do it through a combination of carefully drafted trust language and ongoing financial education. Here are some very creative and powerful elements I have seen added to estate planning documents:

Incentive Trusts

The fear of many parents is that too much money can destroy any ambition and drive that the child may have. Rather than leaving lump sums, parents can use incentives. The "match game" distributes an amount from the trust equal to what the child earns. If Mary makes $150,000 each year as an attorney, the trust will distribute $150,000 to her each year. If her younger sister pours coffee and earns $32,000, she will get $32,000 from the trust.

You could also center distributions on events or accomplishments. You could send $50,000 for graduating college, $100,000 for graduating from a professional school, or $250,000 for earning a PhD. I have seen bonuses for living in a foreign country, having a book published, and even one for completing a marathon.

Some families add language that will ensure distributions to a child who is involved in education or who works for a nonprofit. Maybe you pay a flat fee of $100,000 per year or match the distribution to the highest-earning gainfully employed sibling. You can reward any legal behavior you want.

A Carrot and a Stick

Some families are very concerned that their children not lose sight of how difficult others have it. It is very common for the most successful families to create family foundations. These are private charitable organizations that may be run by family members or non-family members. I have seen a number of trusts that have qualification provisions stating that children must be actively involved in certain foundation operations. Most commonly, I have seen a requirement that children or grandchildren must review grant requests and participate in interviews.

On the other end of the spectrum, I have seen trust provisions that require children to get drug tested routinely. A positive test disqualifies a child from distributions, but does provide funds for the child to get professional treatment.

Strategy No. 4: Protect Your Inheritance from Divorce

When your children or grandchildren come to you, giddy with excitement, and tell you about their engagements, the last thing they want to hear you ask is, "Are you going to sign a prenuptial agreement?" The mistake is not that you want to protect your child. The problem is not that half of marriages end in divorce. The inexcusable faux pas is that you think the only way to protect your inheritance from your child's future ex-spouse is with a prenuptial agreement.

This is just plain wrong. You can still protect your children's inheritances without upsetting your entire family dynamic. If you weren't paying for the wedding, you might lose your invitation for asking such a silly (and completely reasonable, in my opinion) question. Instead, consider leaving assets to your children's irrevocable trusts, with the appropriate spendthrift provisions. Don't give them money outright. Allow your child and the spouse to borrow money from your child's trust for homes, cars, and to start new businesses. Then, if they get divorced, the two of them will each owe money back to your family's trust. That protects your child from getting the shaft—and it doesn't require any signature of approval from your child. Win!

■ **CASE STUDY**

Al and Peg

To illustrate this point, college sweethearts Al and Peg got married right after graduation. Within a few years, their romance turned sour and Al could no longer handle the physical and emotional abuse. During their three-year marriage, Peg received a sizeable inheritance and used it to pay off the couple's mortgage. When they filed for divorce, Al's attorney successfully argued that Al's time and labor on the house, and the fact that he lived in it except when Peg occasionally kicked him out and he had to stay with his mother, made half of the equity in the home, or $100,000, Al's fair share. Though Al and all of his friends will argue that the $100,000 was a small consolation for what he had endured, Peg's grandparents certainly didn't intend for Al to receive their inheritance.

What could Peg have done differently to ensure that she protected her assets? Her grandparents could have left her the inheritance through an irrevocable trust that allowed her to take out only so much money per year. In that case, she would have used the interest from the inheritance to pay the mortgage down each month. If she had done so, the corpus of the inheritance would have remained separate property and would not have been part of the divorce settlement. In the three short years of Al and Peggy's marriage, they would have had nearly zero equity in their home and Al would have left the marriage with the property that he had brought into it, and his wounded pride—but none of Peg's grandparents' life savings.

The bottom line is that we want to give our children every chance at happiness. We don't want the money that we leave them to be motivation for our children's spouses to give up on their marriages. With some clever planning, you can eliminate the risk of your success's threatening your children's long-term happiness, without limiting their ability to benefit from your hard work. Isn't this what we are all trying to do—inspire and protect our heirs? Now that you know that your money doesn't have to hurt your children, let's explore the most powerful way that your financial success can help them.

Strategy No. 5: Be Your Family's Bank— the Billionaire's Secret

The most valuable things you can leave your family are your knowledge, experience, and guidance. The next most valuable thing you can leave them is *access* to money. This strategy is the billionaire's secret. I know this to be true because I have worked on this strategy with two billionaire families in the past year alone. You do not have to be a billionaire to make this work for you, but you will feel like one when you see how powerful it can be.

In chapter 2, you learned how having money significantly helps the successful make even more money. This strategy doesn't work just for people who have money. The most successful families find a way to leverage their money for the benefit of the younger generations. This goes way beyond paying for the best schools and using their connections to get the kids and grandchildren great jobs. The wealthiest families find ways to move hundreds of millions of dollars (or more) with little to no friction. Whenever I say this in a seminar, someone asks, "If estate tax rates have recently been between 40 and 60 percent, how can they pass so much wealth?" That's a good question, deserving of a great answer!

The simple answer is, super affluent families don't pay estate taxes. We live in the golden age of estate planning. Interest rates are very low. The IRS allows related parties (such as employers and employees, parents and children, etc.) to enter into loans or investment arrangements at very low rates. In September 2017, the long-term applicable federal rate was 2.58%. This means that loans of more than nine years could be set at an interest rate of 2.58%. Is this a big deal? Consider this:

■ **CASE STUDY**

The Pewterschmidt Family

The Pewterschmidts are a fictitious famous billionaire family. The matriarch and patriarch, Barbara and Carter, decide that they want to help their grandchildren achieve as much wealth as possible for the benefit of future generations. They lend the dynasty trust $1 billion to purchase the family business. The term of the loan is a 3% interest-only payment until Carter and Barbara pass away. At that time, the principal will be due.

The trust uses the $1 billion loan proceeds to buy the family business. This amount is supported by a third-party valuation firm's estimate and by a recent buyout offer from an unrelated third party. After the purchase by the trust, the business continues doing well, throwing off $160 million of income annually. The trust uses the $160 million in profit to pay off the $30 million in interest payments. The rest of the after-tax profits grows for the benefit of future generations.

Over the 40-year term of the loan, the trust accumulates over $4 billion in estate-tax-free assets. The $1 billion loan is definitely subject to estate taxes when the grandparents pass away. However, the long-term nature of the loan generates a very significant present value discount. The valuation of loans like that is outside the scope of the book, but it can be in excess of 80% in some cases.

The benefit of being your own bank for your family is that it offers you the greatest possible financial leverage. When you own (or want to purchase) assets that you expect to grow at 5% to 10% (or more) per year, you can lend funds at very low rates so that your family wealth grows at an exponential rate outside your taxable estate. When this strategy has been structured correctly, I have seen it save families hundreds of millions of dollars. When done incorrectly, as with the estate planning of the famous Ilitch family (owner of Little Caesar's, the Detroit Tigers, and the Detroit Red Wings), it can result in an enormous estate tax assessment!

Strategy No. 6: Inspire Them with Your Story

When you reach your amazing goals and accumulate extraordinary wealth, you don't just want to pass on family financial wealth. You also want to tell your unique and inspirational story so you pass on family values along with it. You are not only the creator of the family's financial prosperity, but you also likely have a strong desire to provide for the stewardship of the wealth for generations to come. This is no joke.

> *Surveys consistently show that less than 30% of family wealth or family business is retained through the second generation, less than 18% is retained at the end of the third generation, and less than 3% is retained through four generations.*

Consider again the saying mentioned a few times previously: "A rich man's son is seldom a rich man's father." Another adage about wealthy families is that they go "shirtsleeves to shirtsleeves in three generations"—meaning working class to wealthy, then back to working class. Unfortunately, the most successful seldom pass along the appreciation for the wealth or the work ethic for future generations to earn it for themselves.

This is your chance to do it your way (apologies to Frank Sinatra). You can tell your story or let your heirs read about it in the press. I highly suggest hiring a family wealth counselor. I had no idea that these people even existed until I joined a study group. In my group were two amazing family wealth counselors, Doug Hostetler (Maryland) and George Hester (Mississippi). They had such a warmth and calmness about themselves and a clarity around what they brought their clients.

While working with a hardworking, very affluent family in Austin, I brought in Doug Hostetler to help the family get over some of its emotional concerns and complicated family dynamics. What I witnessed was truly extraordinary. Doug asked questions that I never would have thought of asking. He seemed to connect with both the husband and wife on a level I had never witnessed. He was able to help them identify the most important lessons they had learned from parents and grandparents. More important, he helped them communicate what their wildest dreams and deepest fears were for their children and grandchildren. I don't want to get all mushy, but there were lots of tears shed in our meetings—and that was a great thing!

By hiring a family wealth counselor to help you dig a little deeper and to clarify the real issues, you will be better prepared to teach future generations the what, the how, and the why of the family. They will be better prepared to make good stewardship decisions over long periods of time. Families develop a single-mindedness about making value-based decisions.

You have done so much. Your story is amazing. Get a professional to interview you and your spouse, your siblings, your parents. Get a family story put together for future generations. Create a family mission statement. Let your family read your story in your words, not in someone else's. Help them understand what you did, why you did it, how you did it, and what you hope for all of them. It may be the single most powerful thing you can do for your heirs. The best part of it all? You can likely do the whole thing for $10,000 to $15,000.

Category B: Help Others (Now or Later)

There are many different motivations for leaving wealth to a charitable organization. Some of you may have a strong emotional connection to a particular social purpose. This could be educational, religious, societal, or environmental. Others are focused on the tax efficiency that a philanthropic component can add to an overall estate plan. Lastly, some families see charity as the lesser of two evils—as they are already uncomfortable with the amount of wealth they will leave their children and grandchildren.

Regardless of whom you designate as your most deserving interest groups, I want to help you maximize the value they can derive from your efforts. The 2016 US Trust Study of High Net Worth Philanthropy reported that wealthy donors gave to an average of 11 different organizations, while affluent donors under the age of 50 still gave to five charitable causes. The process of determining who gets to benefit from your success, how much each entity will get, and how best to structure each gift can be a full-time job. For many families, it actually is.

To simplify the process, I offer you three categories of gifts. These categories range from the easiest to the most complex. Easiest structures often have the least amount of restrictions and administrative hassles. Some options are more complex, but they offer a wider range of opportunities for leverage. These three categories are:

1. Designating donors
2. Building a foundation
3. Partnering with purpose

Designating Donors

Every person reading this book should know why a will is an inadequate estate planning tool. You should all have a living trust with a pour-over will. If this comes as a surprise to you, or this confuses you, please go to www.jarvistower.com/resources and download the free "Secrets to Estate Planning" document. You may add language to your living trust to designate a portion of your ultimate estate to charities. This is called a bequest. It is also referred to as a "testamentary" or "future" gift. The most common types of testamentary gifts are done through beneficiary designations. Some people name charities as the beneficiaries or contingent beneficiaries of life insurance policies and retirement plans (or IRAs). Each type of gift has pros and cons.

Pros. The beauty of a testamentary or future gift is that you can change it at any time. You can change the amount, the timing and the composition of the gift. This gives you the most flexibility possible. In the case of the gift of an IRA or a retirement plan, there is great leverage. These assets would be taxed at ordinary income tax rates and possibly at estate tax rates—which could deplete 70% of the funds. When retirement plan assets are left to charities, 100% of the funds will be utilized for social benefit. This is the most powerful beneficiary designation you can make.

Cons. By gifting assets at death, your estate will receive a credit against estate planning tax liabilities. However, you will not get to realize the income tax deduction that you could have received if you had made the gift during your earning years.

Building a Foundation

If you want to take advantage of potential income tax benefits and you want to teach your children how to become good stewards of the estate you left for them, you should seriously consider creating a family foundation. A family foundation is a private entity that qualifies for tax treatment as a not-for-profit organization. This is different from a public charity, like the United Way, the Red Cross, or a public university. Here are six reasons why family foundations are in favor with the most successful, and why you should consider them.

1. **Tax deduction today. Make a decision tomorrow.** Funds paid to your foundation are tax-deductible. Only 5% of the funds must be paid to a public charity each year. If you aren't sure which group should get your money, or you want your children involved in that decision-making process, this benefit is powerful.

2. **Make a name for your family.** By creating a foundation, you show the world that you are very serious about your philanthropic endeavors. There is a certain gravitas that comes with a foundation. This may afford you or your family increased access to other serious philanthropists who may share your goals.

3. **Eliminate unwanted solicitations.** When you have a foundation, you can direct solicitors to the family foundation, its specific giving areas, and its mission statement. This allows you to politely turn down requests that don't fit your goals. If you have a specific set of causes or mission statement, this can also help you connect with other foundations, donors, and philanthropists who share your feelings for certain causes.

4. **Strengthen your family bonds.** Your family trusts (discussed in the fifth secret) may require family members to participate in the family foundation. While they are involved in the foundation, they may participate in philanthropic research, review applications for grants, present their findings to other family members on the board of the foundation, and participate in the decision-making process. Over time, they will review the results of their results and learn which gifts make a greater impact. If your family members wish to be successful in industry, the skills learned while working on the board of the foundation will be valuable.

5. **Donation flexibility.** A private foundation allows your family to provide emergency assistance directly to individuals using dollars for which you've already received a tax deduction. This could help you to help others who may not qualify under any specific charity. To take it a step further, you could help other organizations (not just people). Some new programs in your area may provide a wonderful benefit to those in need, but they may not have been created as nonprofit organizations. Direct charitable activities are IRS-approved programs that permit foundations to directly fund and carry out their own projects.

6. **Financial flexibility.** Your foundation may pay legitimate and reasonable expenses incurred in carrying out its charitable mission. These will count toward the annual minimum distribution requirement. Foundations can also provide loans instead of grants. When used to support a charitable purpose, loans, loan guarantees, and even equity investments, which are paid back (potentially with interest), can be employed by private foundations. This can help your foundation to replenish your philanthropic capital for future charitable causes.

If you are interested in three or more of these six benefits, then you may want to consider creating a family foundation to supplement your long-term estate planning and to enhance the legacy you leave. If you are interested in only one or two of these benefits, you might be able to meet your goals by creating a donor-advised fund or a pooled income fund. These may allow you to accomplish those goals without all the cost and maintenance of starting your own foundation.

There are some very interesting legal tools you may want to consider if you are considering splitting a gift between your favorite charities and your favorite family members. Charitable gift annuities, charity lead trusts, and charitable remainder trusts allow you to separate access to income during your lifetime and use of the assets after you pass away. I don't have time to go into all of these options in this book. Luckily, the planned giving departments of most major universities and larger charities have robust libraries of materials available online. In the final few pages of this book, I want to share some very innovative strategies for the philanthropic-minded among you who would love to create a game-changing endowment for generations to come.

Changing the Game: Partnering with a Purpose

For those of you who really want to do something different for your favorite not-for-profit organization, you need to really elevate your perspective. This is the most passionate part of this book for me. I believe I have an interesting perspective, having sat on a number of nonprofit advisory boards and having donated to over 25 charities. I have committed more than a million dollars each to my two alma maters, my national fraternity, and my magnet high school. Every one of these groups has a need for money. Each one of them has amazing vision. All of them have detailed plans for how to use the funds to make the world a better place.

Having a deserving purpose, a clear vision, and dedicated donors is not enough. Charitable, educational, and religious organizations have an increased need for private funding. Despite the need for increased donations, each donor has multiple concerns and a limited amount of money. The 2017 US Trust Study of High Net Worth Philanthropy also pointed out that 17% of donors stopped giving because they were tired of receiving too many solicitations. It's an interesting catch-22 for organizations. If you don't ask, you won't receive. If you ask too often, you might be cut off. Those of us who care about our favorite causes *must* think very differently about raising money or we may fail to survive.

What I am going to share next is a set of innovative solutions I came up with when a client of mine asked me to meet with his alma mater. I consulted with a major state university's medical school to provide ideas on how to compete with the largest educational and healthcare institutions. Rather than take these ideas and market them directly myself, I am offering them to you so you can learn from them. Perhaps you will take the same idea to help your beloved alma mater. Maybe you will use these strategies to help solve the social problem that hurts your heart most. If you want assistance, I encourage you to contact my firm. This is our favorite part of what we do.

JarvisTower Five-Part Program for University X

1. **80/20 plan.** We offer educational seminars for key donors. We show attendees multiple ways to significantly reduce expenses, improve profitability, or increase the value of their businesses. We encourage attendees to donate 20% of the savings or earnings they get out of the seminar to the university. If any of the attendees hire us, we donate 20% of our collections to the charity.

2. **Insure Success (the fourth secret).** We created a licensed insurance agency for the university. This allows us to help the client to reduce the net cost of healthcare, property, and liability insurance expenses. The recurring revenue for the organization can be used to endow an academic chair or to hire the replacement for a coach on the hot seat.

3. **Transform expenses to endowment (nonprofit TrEE).** Many institutions of higher education, including the University of Michigan, have famously employed (pun intended) creative

alternative compensation agreements. The philosophy is to turn expenses into assets for the institution. We have worked on these structures for entities that employ physicians, for high-profile coaches, and for presidents and deans of universities. Imagine turning every bonus or incentive into a loan that would be repaid to the university or hospital at some defined point in the future. This is explained in greater detail in the fifth secret.

4. **Infinite endowment.** With our knowledge of the insurance industry, we decided to work with an innovative insurance company to devise a specialty insurance program for all students, faculty, and alumni. This allows all of them to secure insurance without a medical exam while they are students or employees of the system. When the insured people leave, they can leave the death benefit to the university as a gift (to create an endowment) or transfer the policy to themselves (generating a commission for the university).

5. **Billion-dollar plan.** We are working on a second proprietary insurance offering for all nonprofit organizations. Employed people or donors of a certain age may apply for insurance without a medical exam, provided they designate all or part of the death benefit for the charity. Our goal is to secure 1,000 commitments from donors who would donate a $1 million insurance death benefit.

These strategies may or may not make sense for your particular cause. The point of sharing these ideas is to stimulate you to think differently in your attempt to find that elevated perspective. When you achieve the better viewpoint, you will see better ways to help your organization succeed. This is no different than what you have been doing for yourself throughout the book. The only difference is that you are now turning your attention toward making sure that your generous donations of time and money benefit from the same important leverage.

See a Better Path

You spent 85% of this book working on how to achieve your desired level of success. You began by defining what success means for you. You learned how to achieve the right mindset for success. Then you looked at ways to structure your business, your assets, and your advisors to maximize the leverage you need to beat the odds. In the sixth secret, you finally learned how important it is to ask yourself why you are working so hard.

When you achieve your ambitious goals, you will realize a very significant level of wealth. You are more than likely to have far more than you will ever spend. What are you going to do with that money? What legacy are you going to leave for your heirs, your community, and the rest of the world?

In the 2016 US Trust Study of High Net Worth Philanthropy, 70% of wealthy donors surveyed stated that their primary goal was to leave wealth for their family. You may want to leave money for future generations, but you undoubtedly don't want to leave it in ways that could have a negative impact. Dynasty trusts allow you to leave money for multiple generations. Spendthrift provisions in a trust can eliminate the need for prenuptial agreements. His-and-hers trusts can move $11 million (plus all growth) out of your estate while giving you access. Families worth $25 million to $2.5 billion benefit greatly from being their own "family bank."

Though the majority of families want to leave money primarily to their heirs, 91% of high-net-worth families surveyed by US Trust make annual donations to charity. Of those, 83% expected to give as much or more the following year. This is a very positive outlook for charitable organizations, especially as government funding appears to be diminishing substantially with the current administration. Undoubtedly, the gifting outlook is positive because there are so many creative ways to structure gifts. Whether you are making beneficiary designations for your retirement plans or for your life insurance policies, every gift does count.

You may choose to utilize some combination of advanced estate planning and a family foundation. This can create the scenario of a zero estate tax liability while providing a mechanism for your heirs to stay involved in helping others who are less fortunate than they are. Many creative trust provisions can be integrated with the infinitely important and equally powerful family mission statement that I recommend for every "new money" family. These valuable lessons can help your family accept the stewardship that comes with significant wealth.

Lastly, you can take an active role in fundraising and endowment building with an educational, religious, or community service organization. We would love to help you build annuity-producing programs that would ensure long-term survival and thriving for generations to come. All of this is an important part of your legacy building. Please continue to the concluding chapter for some final words of wisdom as you embark on your better path to success.

CHAPTER 9

Follow the Better Path—Now

"If not us, who? If not now, when?"

—John F. Kennedy

During my twenty-five years of consulting, I have become increasingly discouraged and fed up with the financial services industry, the professional service firms, and the infrastructure-heavy business landscape. It has become difficult for a business owner to create any real value for society without being overwhelmed by compliance, regulations, infrastructure, rules, restrictions, "must-dos" and "must-haves." Every firm and industry would get its pound of flesh from businesses as soon as they became successful (if not sooner). The creative lifeblood was being sucked from the marrow of would-be entrepreneurs.

When I did the economic research, it was no surprise that it was so difficult to get to the highest levels of success. What was most interesting was what I learned from talking with Professor Art Markman (human dimension of organizations, University of Texas at Austin) and Professor Axel Anderson (economics, Georgetown University). You just can't achieve success with labor alone. You can't be super successful without some luck. You definitely can't achieve great affluence while trying to fit in. You need luck. You need leverage. You can't be afraid of failing.

What has helped my wealthiest clients be successful is the ability to embrace and prepare for failure. They all have inner strength to help them ignore all the criticism and worry others have for them. They have all avoided catastrophe while taking much greater risk. All of the positive-mindset lessons herein are provided to give you some motivation to help you get through whatever is holding you back.

The practical strategies for protecting assets, creating leverage, building new income sources, reducing risks, empowering people, and leaving a legacy are suggestions. You may use some of them. You may use none of them. The goal is to get you to think about things in a different way. I am trying to get you to elevate your perspective, so you can see a better path to your success. This is your perspective, your path, your success.

I want to inspire you to find what success means to you. This book has given you some tips on how to do it faster so that the "when" will be even sooner than you might think. Perhaps I have made you think about why you are working so hard. Perhaps the ideas in the sixth secret will help you leave a better, longer-lasting legacy.

My "why" is that I want to give business owners, wealthy families, and their professional advisors my best ideas. I want to show you how to circumvent the institutions that are taking advantage of business owners. I want to show you a better path to success—that doesn't involve making everybody else rich along the way. I want to give creative people a better chance to just be creative. Am I projecting what I want for myself? Absolutely. Is that a bad thing? Only you can be the judge of that. Hopefully, this book has given you a few ideas that will really help you, your family, your employees, and your business.

Additional Resources

To minimize paper waste, to ensure that the ever-changing content is kept fresh and up to date, and to improve the effectiveness of the exercise worksheets, the resources below can be found at www.JarvisTower.com/resources.

- Resource A: Setting *Your* Ambitious Goals
- Resource B: How to Assess Threats to *Your* Personal Economy
- Resource C: The Pros and Cons of Property and Casualty Insurance
- Resource D: Limited Liability Companies and Limited Partnerships
- Resource E: Your Personal Sanctuary—the 678 Trust
- Resource F: Are Your Advisors Working for You or Against You?
- Resource G: Seven Ways Not to Hire Advisors
- Resource H: Full Perspective Form
- Resource I: Seminar Request Form
- Resource J: Consulting Request Form

All readers will receive free access to these and other resources, as well as our newsletter.